DIANA
AN AMAZING LIFE
THE PEOPLE COVER STORIES 1981-1997

CONTENTS

“ **The welcome news pealed through Britain last week that the world's most eligible bachelor had, at 32, plighted his troth to 19-year-old Lady Diana Spencer . . .**

—PEOPLE'S MARCH 9, 1981, STORY ABOUT CHARLES'S ENGAGEMENT FIRST MENTIONED HIS FIANCEE, A SHY KINDERGARTEN TEACHER, ON LINE 19

ON FEB. 24, 1981, Buckingham Palace announced that Prince Charles, 32, who for years had seemed to be approaching the altar from an oblique angle, had become engaged. Although the British press had covered his burgeoning romance for months, American magazines and TV had paid little attention. PEOPLE's story about the announcement—two pages in the March 9, 1981 issue—talked of Charles's and England's joy and first mentioned the name of his fiancée, Lady Diana Spencer, 19, in the second paragraph.

It was, figuratively if not literally, the last time she would receive second billing.

Over the next 16 years, Lady Diana—who that summer became Princess Diana—appeared on more covers of PEOPLE than any person before or since. This book contains the 42 covers that focused on Diana's world and told the story of her life, as it was presented in PEOPLE, from June 22, 1981 until Sept. 22, 1997. The headlines, captions and selected text and pictures are, in almost every chapter, exactly as they originally appeared in the magazine.

The goal of this book isn't to analyze her life, but to re-create, in a small way, something of what those 16 years felt like. A decade later, it still doesn't seem quite believable.

Could it all really have happened just that way?

PART ONE

THE FAIRY TALE

"She needs everything a newlywed needs. Sofas for the living room and wooden spoons for the kitchen

—an aide to the Queen, on Lady Diana's upcoming wedding

John Lennon

Susan Ford as
a mellow mom

*Hazzard's ham,
James Best*

Designer jean ripoffs

The bizarre life of a killer

JUNE 22, 1981 ■ 95¢

People
weekly

LADY DIANA

**A sneak preview
of her Big Day:
the wedding gowns
(all 6 of them!),
the gifts, guests
and the royal pain
of planning
it all**

Preparing for her fairy-tale wedding puts Lady Di in a royal tizzy

JUST A GIRL," marveled a pedigreed English gentleman after he shared a box at Covent Garden with Lady Diana Spencer. Ah, but sir, look closer, beyond that shyly downturned chin and those blushing cheeks the color of an English tea rose. The 19-year-old who next month becomes the Princess of Wales is a seasoned veteran of the highest society, and as the daughter of Earl Spencer she grew up calling the Queen of England "Aunt Lillibet." If all that—plus months of evading a king-size plague of photographers—has not suitably matured her, then planning for her July 29 wedding surely will. Lady Di is cast in the lead of a pageant that will be viewed by 600 million global TV watchers, a spectacle whose pomp and complicated circumstance will register on the extravaganza scale somewhere between the original parting of the Red Sea and Cecil B. De Mille's reconstruction of it.

Lady Di plays Princess Charming at a tree-planting ceremony in Hampshire in memory of Prince Charles's great-uncle Lord Mountbatten. "I'll just have to get used to the backs of photographers when she is near me," quipped the prince.

Guarding her left hand with its $60,000
sapphire-and-diamond engagement ring,
Di proffers her right in Gloucester.

EIIR

The Lord Chamberlain is Commanded by
The Queen and The Duke of Edinburgh to invite

to the Marriage of
His Royal Highness The Prince of Wales
with
The Lady Diana Spencer
in St. Paul's Cathedral
on Wednesday, 29th July, 1981 at 11.00 a.m.

An answer is requested to the Lord Chamberlain,
St. James's Palace, London, S.W.1.

Dress: Uniform, Morning Dress
or Lounge Suit.

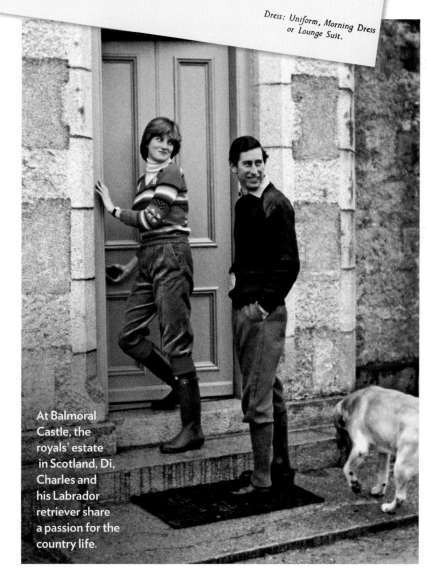

At Balmoral Castle, the royals' estate in Scotland, Di, Charles and his Labrador retriever share a passion for the country life.

"Here is the stuff of which fairy tales are made

—the Archbishop of Canterbury

AUGUST 3, 1981 ■ 95¢

People weekly

...ves in
on Wayne Newton
**Beverly Hills Diet:
Can it kill you?**
Brazil gags Baez

GOOD SHOW!

**Behind the pageantry
a handful of loyal subjects
gives a magic touch
to the fairy-tale
wedding**

Once upon a time of trouble, a Cinderella wed her fella and dreary old England made merrie once more

THE ROYAL WEDDING

LOVELY AS
THE SUMMER MORN

The bride shone brightly in a pearl-encrusted gown made from 40 yards of ivory taffeta silk spun at the royal silkworm farm. Charles, smashing in his full dress Royal Navy uniform, with blue Order of the Garter sash and decorations glistening on his tunic, didn't look bad himself. But Di did the dazzling. Her (future) Majesty's dress, hand-stitched with vintage lace trim and trailing a 25-ft. train, was created by David and Elizabeth Emanuel. The design remained a state secret until the princess-to-be rode to her nuptials in—what else?—a glass coach.

I
N A DISPLAY of pageantry and an outpouring of jubilation unseen on the sceptred isle since the sun set on her empire, as many as a million Britons ignored terror threats, troubles in Ireland and strife in the streets to witness what seemed a fairy tale come true. With some 750 million viewers worldwide glued to their tellys, Prince Charles, the 32-year-old heir to the throne of England, took as his bride the radiant Lady Diana Spencer, 20. A Chuck-struck schoolgirl who once slept with Charles's picture by her bed, the former kindergarten teacher wowed the vast throngs who raised thunderous cheers as she and her groom led a procession of gilded horse-drawn carriages from St. Paul's Cathedral to Buckingham Palace. Although Princess Grace of Monaco was among the many crowned and titled personages on hand, the newlyweds displayed a deft commoner's touch. Hung from the trunk of the sumptuous coach that carried them off on their honeymoon was a hand-scrawled "JUST MARRIED!" sign certain to stop traffic on the road to happily ever after.

EDITOR'S NOTE

This section contains photos that did not run in the original cover story. That's because—an astounding fact—PEOPLE ran no wedding pictures at the time of the wedding. Why? The ceremony took place hours after that week's issue went to press; in order to have something wedding-related on the newsstand in the following days, the editors elected to run a story about the army of bakers, stylists and courtiers who made the extravagant ceremony possible (see page 88). Most of the pictures here first ran in the magazine years later.

THE WEDDING PARTY
Before they could dig into the 168-lb. cake, the wedding party posed for a formal portrait: (from left) Edward van Cutsem, Catherine Cameron, Lord Nicholas Windsor, Sarah-Jane Gaselee, India Hicks, Prince Edward; Charles; Diana; Prince Andrew; Lady Sarah Chatto and Clementine Hambro.

HERE COMES HER HIGHNESS

It took the bride-to-be four minutes to walk the 330-ft. aisle to the altar. After exchanging vows (omitting the traditional bridal promise to obey), she made the return trip on the arm of her husband. Preparing for a photo session with her attendants after the ceremony (right), Diana—with her newly minted mum-in-law, the Queen, looking on—comforted her youngest bridesmaid, Clementine Hambro. The bride knew her maid well: Clementine was one of Diana's kindergarten students.

WEDDING JITTERS

The epitome of elegant splendor, the wedding wasn't without it's missteps: A flustered Diana called the Prince "Philip Charles Arthur George" instead of "Charles Philip Arthur George," while the prince neglected to mention the word "worldly" as he pledge to share all of his worldly goods with his bride.

BALCONY BUSS With as many as a quarter of a million people below their Buckingham Palace balcony shouting "Kiss her!" the Prince and Princess obliged.

A NATION OF SHOPKEEPERS, BAKERS AND LACEMAKERS STAGED A GRAND ROYAL WEDDING

COACHMAN RICHARD BOLAND praised the temperament of Lady Penelope, one of two bays assigned to Lady Di's carriage. He and his team, he says, "take any procession in stride."

LEPIDOPTERIST ROBERT GOODDEN got his worms going early and provided the silk for the bridal gown. His company, Lullingstone, did the same for Queen Elizabeth in 1947.

ROYAL NAVY BAKER DAVID AVERY planned to escape to Scotland for some needed R & R. "I'll play golf," he says, "and lose myself for a week."

CHIEF CHORISTER GEOFFREY TAYLOR and 37 St. Paul's schoolmates provided the vocals for many parts of the wedding service. Leaving nothing to chance, Prince Charles chose the music.

PART TWO

THE LITTLE PRINCES

> **"British princes are taught humility through a routine of sensible clothes, few parties and very dull meals**

—*Royal Children* author Celia Clear

Ed Asner Hollywood's ...boss

Exclusive: a talk with that ex-CIA agent in Libya

Mary Martin is back

Happy Days' **happy hour**

NOVEMBER 23, 1981 ▪ 95¢

People
weekly

The Pregnant Princess

Nannies, nappies, names and Lord knows what all: Di and Charles plan for the royal heir

0 10227

47

724414

Wonder What the British Royal Heir Will Look Like?

Mom and Pop as babies give a clue

Will the new heir be a spectacular blonde like 1-year-old Diana (left) or will England toast a lad as handsome as Charles at 5 months?

I T SEEMED AS though the rice had hardly been swept off the steps of St. Paul's before Britain was proudly atwitter over a new royal announcement: The newlywed Diana, Princess of Wales, is expecting to deliver an heir to the throne sometime in June. After a brief pause during which "the nation's mums counted on their fingers," as one wry observer put it, the Buckingham Palace switchboard was jammed with congratulatory calls, hundreds of well-wishers gathered at the gates, and Fleet Street hailed the WONDERFUL NEWS in banner headlines.

The blessed event, if all goes well, will occur a prompt if perfectly proper 11 months after the July 29 wedding.

Diana was a tad queasy at a museum party the night before the Nov. 5 announcement. She left early.

66 **The baby is lucky to have Diana as a mother. I'm off to have a beer**

—Earl Spencer, Diana's father, upon the birth of his royal grandson

MARIE OSMOND & a bouquet of celeb brides

JULY 5, 1982 ■ $1.00

People weekly

OH, BOY!

For Diana's
7-pound,
1½-ounce
prince,
the palace
plans
a future
fit for
a king

Diana and Charles carried the day-old prince home from the hospital. "He has the good fortune," said Charles, "not to look like me."

A ROYAL TREAT FOR ENGLAND

Thoroughly modern birth adds a chapter to the storybook life of Diana and Charles

THE 41-GUN salute at the Tower of London and Hyde Park signaled a king for the 21st century. The huzzahs rose across Britain, and eyes misted over from Land's End to John o'Groats. Well-wishers pressed to the gates of Buckingham Palace to read the placard that royal assistants hung out for the world to see last Monday eve: "Her Royal Highness the Princess of Wales was safely delivered of a son at 9:03 p.m. today. Her Royal Highness and her child are both doing well."

The 7-lb. 1½-oz. prince is expected someday to rule the United Kingdom. He has already commandeered the

attention of his future subjects from such concerns as the Falklands and Wimbledon. Even the newborn's father, normally the most serious of men, was transported. Charles, said his father-in-law, was "absolutely over the moon."

"He's very well, but very noisy

—Charles on his newborn son William

AUGUST 16, 1982 ∎$1.00

People weekly

Sinatra, R.J. Wagner,
Jill St. John and Carson
open an L.A. showplace

Facts of Life in Paris

Broadway's X-rated star

KING OF HEARTS

**A royal christening—
and a touching
moment for Diana
and her little prince**

0 10227

33

724414

In his gala palace debut, little William takes his place in a noble and eccentric line

I T WAS A brief ceremony for His Royal Highness Prince William Arthur Philip Louis of Wales—but then it was only the first of thousands. The very first official pronouncements of the infant who is expected to one day be King of England were the three little squeaks he emitted in the Music Room of Buckingham Palace as Dr. Robert Runcie, the Archbishop of Canterbury, poured the baptismal water over his head. Although medieval Britons believed that such cries were a sign that the Devil had left the child's body, Diana still blushed at each squeal, Prince Charles gallantly wiped dribbles from his son's chin, and Queen Elizabeth later joked that her grandson showed stage presence: "He's a good speechmaker."

In a palace session, Princess Margaret's ex, Lord Snowdon, snapped this first glimpse of the new parents and child.

A CONQUEROR, A CAD, A CALVINIST AND A PHILANDERER: THAT'S WHAT'S IN THE NAME YOUNG PRINCE WILLIAM HAS INHERITED

HASTINGS AND HARD LOVE

The tradition of royal Williams in England begins with the country's Norman Conqueror, who sets the present prince an example of valor, if not of good manners. The bastard son of the Duke of Normandy, William had united the province under him by age 20 and did the same in England after defeating King Harold at Hastings in 1066. Though a just king, William was not a pleasant person. It is said he wooed his wife, Matilda of Flanders, by dragging her around her room by her hair. Insulted by the inhabitants of one town he was besieging, he lopped off the hands and feet of 32 of its citizens and tossed them over its walls. Like Matilda, the town gave in.

WILLIAM THE WORST

He was William I's favorite son, but William Rufus was a monarch only a father could love. A stammering, bull-necked blond with eyes of different colors, he engaged in what chroniclers of the day called "unnatural vices," feuded with the church and ravaged the lands and pocketbooks of his subjects. Killed by an arrow shot by one of his men, he was buried in the then-new Winchester Cathedral, one of whose towers collapsed on his grave.

"Now I'm going to blow my nose for everyone to photograph

—Charles to relentless press corps

JANUARY 31 1983

EDDIE MURPHY: a millionaire

JANUARY 31, 1983 ∎ $1.25

People
weekly

The Doles: D.C.'s
power couple

Andy Gibb: fired

Glen Campbell:
now Wife No. 4

DIANA'S ORDEAL

The pressures of
being a princess
build to an
Alpine holiday
face-off

"Why don't you leave us alone? Why don't you go away?" Diana asked photographers who pursued her down the slopes.

Diana's reticence upset the usually imperturbable prince. Predicted a London columnist: "There will be more strain on Charles."

PRINCESS DIANA'S ROYAL RETREAT

During an Alpine ski holiday disrupted by the press, she displays a renewed zeal for privacy

THE TROUBLE STARTED even before the royal couple arrived. Buckingham Palace had not briefed reporters on the destination of the Prince and Princess of Wales, who, like thousands of British couples, were taking a January ski vacation in the Alps. But the Queen's plane had barely touched down in Zurich, Switzerland, on Sunday, Jan. 9, when a local reporter played a hunch and phoned the residence (above) of Prince Franz Josef in Liechtenstein, the tiny principality just across the border. "What will happen when Prince Charles stays with you this week?" asked the reporter. Came the astonished and tattletale reply: "How did you find out?"

For Diana, 21, what was supposed to have been a private getaway (with 7-month-old baby William in a nanny's care in England) turned rapidly into a public spectacle. Tailed by an aggressive press that was unshackled by palace conventions usually respected in Britain, Charles and Diana found themselves caught in a Keystone Kops version of cat-and-mouse. And, as the week-long battle with the press continued, "shy Di" was no longer bashful about her preference for privacy. On and off the slopes, Diana was uncharacteristically icy to the pursuing paparazzi. As she pulled down her ski cap and hid her face behind gloves during one close encounter with the press, even Charles found her behavior frustrating and pleaded, "Please, Diana, don't do that. You're being stupid."

" Royal firstborns may get all the glory, but second-borns enjoy more freedom —Diana

MTM: Her life-threatening battle

OCTOBER 1, 1984 ■ $1.25

People
weekly

Stefanie Powers sizzles in *Mistral's* Family feud for Mr. T

DI'S PRIDE AND JOY

Move over, William—little Prince Henry is checking into the royal nursery

HELLO HARRY!

Britain welcomes another prince to the House of Windsor

OUTSIDE ST. MARY'S Hospital in the slightly shabby London section of Paddington, the crowd was growing by the minute—more than 300 reporters, TV technicians and onlookers milled anxiously behind police barricades and dozens of photographers and TV cameramen perched atop ladders nearby. Inside the hospital, Diana, Princess of Wales, had been in labor since 7:30 a.m. Finally, after nine hours, as the afternoon light began to fade and a gray sky threatened rain, a son emerged for all of Britain. Fair of face and blue-eyed like his brother William, he weighed in at 6 lbs., 14 oz. The infant, third in line to the throne after his father and brother, would be known officially as Prince Henry Charles Albert David, it was announced—and just "Harry" to his family and chums. A TV crewman, hooked up to his home office through headphones, broke the news to the mob outside St. Mary's. "It's a boy!" he shouted. The crowd exploded in cheers. At that, a rubbernecking motorist in front of the hospital drove into the side of an ambulance.

Before Harry's birth, Wills climbed up steps to a waiting plane at Aberdeen airport. At home, says Charles, "he's very destructive."

"Hurrah, Harry!" shouted frenzied well-wishers outside St. Mary's Hospital as a radiant Diana and Charles emerged with their 13-hour-old prince swathed in a blanket.

Police's Sting: a sexy hit in *Dune*

JANUARY 14, 1985 ▪ $1.50

People weekly

HARRY

How his christening fueled the royal feud between Diana and Princess Anne

A WINDSOR WAR

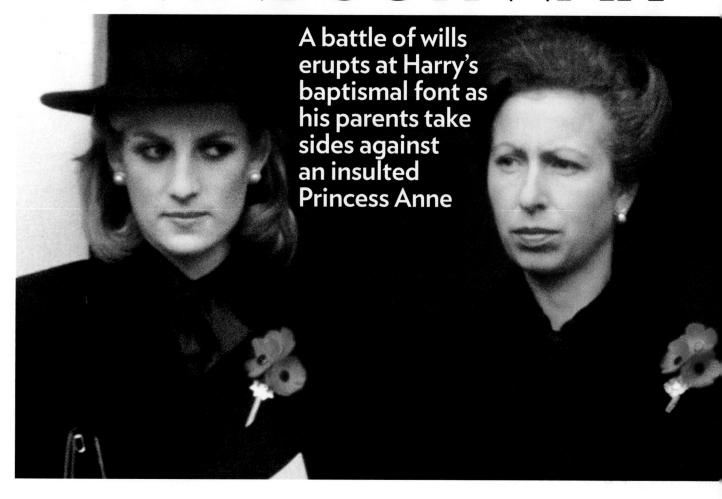

A battle of wills erupts at Harry's baptismal font as his parents take sides against an insulted Princess Anne

At Remembrance Day Services last November, Diana and Anne kept an emotional—if not physical—distance.

"A LL HAPPY FAMILIES are alike, but an unhappy family is unhappy after its own fashion," Count Leo Tolstoy once wrote of Russian aristocracy. But in London at year's end, it was the British royals—once models of at least surface harmony—who seemed woefully besmirched by bad tempers and rifts. In their fashion, of course, they struggled to be mum and mollifying about it all. But nothing could quite hide the rather awkward truth: While 3-month-old Prince Henry Charles Albert David, third in line to the British throne, was ceremoniously baptized over a Victorian gilded lily font by the Archbishop of Canterbury in

St. George's Chapel, Windsor, his Auntie Anne and her husband, Capt. Mark Phillips, were out shooting in the countryside, bagging rabbits.

The real field day, naturally, was in the British press, which turned Anne's "snubbing" of her nephew's christening into an apocalyptic—and apoplectic—event. How, they fumed, could Anne send her children, Peter, 7, and Zara, 3, but stay away herself? A feud in the House of Windsor, rumored for months, had finally erupted for all to see, crowed Fleet Street. Whiffs of grapeshot were first reported last October, when Prince Philip was said to be annoyed with Charles's lack of regard for his sister. Anne, 34, had not been named one of Prince William's six godpar-

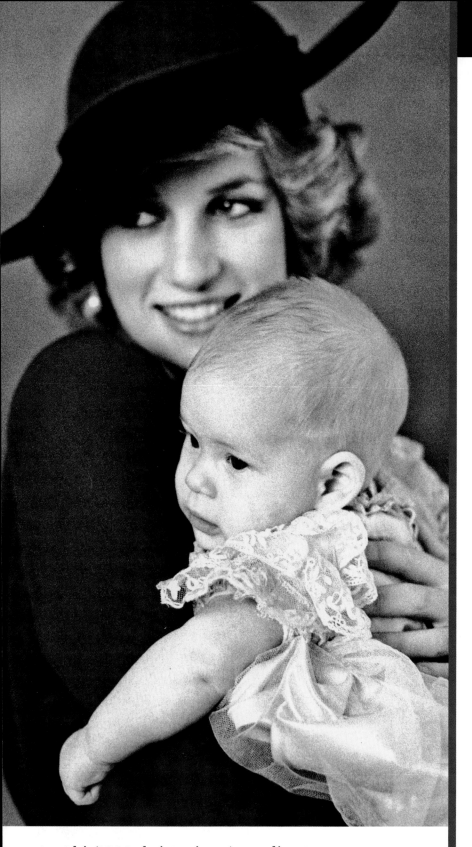

ents at his 1982 christening. According to one senior royal aide, "Prince Philip was very hopeful she would be chosen *this* time." Yet when the list of Harry's godparents was published on Nov. 15, Anne's name was not among them.

THIRTY YEARS A PRINCESS

NOW DON'T YOU feel sorry
for poor Princess Anne
She seems so sincere,
and she stands by her man
But as each year goes by,
through no fault of her own,
She moves another notch
away from the throne

HOW MUST SHE be feeling,
our poor Princess Anne
She's been training for glory
since her life began
Well it's true in the saddle
she's a regular champ
But she's never going to see
her pretty face on a stamp

BUT SHE CAN rise, she can curtsey
and she's quite well-to-do
She can stand up for hours
without going to the loo
But from her place
on the short list
She watched fate intervene
Now it's 30 years a princess
And never a queen

This ditty on Canadian radio by songwriter Nancy White may never play the palace.

"She has brought us a real breath of spring

—Marchese Emilio Pucci, Italian fashion designer who hosted a grand dinner for the royal couple in Florence

MAY 20, 1985 ■ $1.50

People weekly

TALK ABOUT POWER TRIPS!

An inside report on the yacht, the jets, the banquets, the gowns and the gaffes . . .

. . . as Charles & Di & Ron & Nancy do Europe on $1 million a day— at least

0 10227

20

0 724414

DOING EUROPE RIGHT

With princely pomp and presidential power, the Royals and the Reagans—retinues in tow—packed heavy, ate light and saw the sights

T HE TWO MOST famous couples in the world recently descended on Europe within days of each other, and the lessons they learned might be of help to summer travelers abroad. Rule Number One: If you are Prince Charles and Princess Diana, don't worry about anything—you'll eventually charm an entire country, particularly if it's Italy. Rule Number Two: If you're President Ronald Reagan and wife Nancy, why not settle for a nice trip to California?

Dubbed the "anorexic dress" by reporters, this pink frock startled Milan.

Even if the pres said it made her look like an Itali waiter, the suit wore on her tour of Florence was, at least, ne

For a Florence banquet, the princess sported a star-spangled, Spanish-style flamenco dress and got mixed reviews.

David and Elizabeth Emanuel, who made Di's wedding dress, did her Venice outfit. "Coco the clown," said the press.

Though art and architecture are Charles's passions, not Diana's, the Greek theater overlooking the Great Harbor in Syracuse enchanted them both.

CRACKS IN THE AMORE

" Diana will come to understand her life for the sterile existence that it is

—royal watcher Nigel Dempster

JULY 22 1985

10

DURAN DURAN: A romp~~~~rich

JULY 22, 1985 ■ $1.50

People
weekly

MALICE
in the
PALACE

Forget shy Di! Behind this facade is a willful woman who has family servants on the run and who's dancing the night away— sometimes without Charles

REBELLION AT KENSINGTON

FIVE FIRED AIDES

Bodyguard **PAUL OFFICER** had escorted Di. They clashed, and he later left royal service.

Former v turned-a **STEPHE BARRY** sa helped a Charles's liaisons d the princ bachelor

As Prince Charles grows increasingly listless, wife Diana takes charge—and recently departed employees say she's made the palace "a minefield"

MARCH 26: Diana, Princess of Wales, turns up at London's Grosvenor House for a charity gala staged by Bruce Oldfield, one of her favorite designers. Attended only by three "courtiers," she ignores royal protocol by failing to leave at a previously arranged time. Instead she lags behind to dance and chat with beautiful people such as Christopher Reeve and French composer Jean-Michel Jarre.

JUNE 1: Diana, again without Charles, arrives for a Saturday night dance at a friend's country house in Leicestershire. When bashful bachelors are too timid to ask her to dance, she takes matters into her own hands. Grabbing a partner, she exclaims, "Come on, for goodness sake, let's dance!" She does—until 4 a.m.

JUNE 21: Queen Elizabeth hosts a 21st-birthday bash at Windsor for her son Prince Edward and three of his cousins. After a few whirls around the dance floor with his frisky wife, Charles retires to the sidelines. Diana, however, continues to bop to the music alone.

CHARLES AND DIANA WILL celebrate their anniversary on July 29. Yet little more than halfway toward that fabled seven-year itch, there are signs of conflict in the royal household. Diana, no longer the blushing kindergarten teacher who snared the world's most eligible bachelor, is displaying a new assertiveness and self-confidence. She is venturing out socially without Charles more than ever, and this month—for the first time—her public engagements will outnumber his.

Charles sought wifely consolation after a polo team defeat last month. "They call each other darling, and they mean it," says one observer.

The departure of Charles's private secretary **EDWARD ADEANE** "must have been a tragedy for the prince," says one observer.

JOHN BROWNRIDGE last month became the fifth protection officer to leave Charles and Diana's service.

A personality clash between Diana and her private secretary **OLIVER EVERETT** (a pal of Charles's) led to his departure.

North and South's trashy vixen

NOVEMBER 11, 1985 ■ $1.50

People weekly

What's Diana Worth to Britain?

$500,000,000

Plus:
- Charles & Di's London condo
- How she chooses all those clothes

Princess Diana, hood ornament to an empire, may be the best advertisement for Britain since the Beatles

BIRTH OF A SALESWOMAN

O N NOV. 11, Princess Diana, future Queen of England, will awaken at the British Ambassador's residence in Washington, D.C., climb into a limousine and ride south on I-395 to Springfield, Va. Her destination: a suburban mall housing J.C. Penney's. Inside, she'll chat with company executives, smile at the sales staff and pause—with cameras recording her every nod—to admire racks of British-made sweaters, skirts, dresses, coats, shoes and scarves. Not surprisingly, Penney's management is gaga over the anticipated publicity windfall. "It's a whole new ball game for us," says a company spokesman. "Her fresh young image—to be associated with that is invaluable to us.

Quick: What does the top of Diana's head look like? If you can't remember, maybe it's because she wore 27 hats and two tiaras between Feb. 1 and Aug. 1, including (from top) a sleek brown-and-white, a stiff brimmer, a Graham Smith, a Nurse Nancy and a floppy disc. "She has the biggest head size we make," says one milliner.

When the Queen came to this country, she went to Bloomingdale's, but Diana is coming to Penney's. There could not be a better person for us."

Diana, of course, is not visiting Penney's merely out of a desire to see how Americans kill time at a mall. She's going because, in a way, it's her job: Penney's recently purchased $50 million worth of British goods, and Diana is lending her aura to help sell them. Prince Charles himself has said that fostering that aura, creating "a positive atmosphere toward Britain," is one of the major functions of the royals. "I would like to hope that maybe through trying to engender that sort of awareness and interest . . . that other things would follow, like increased trade and export opportunities," he said during the couple's recent British TV interview. "This is an area which, I feel, hasn't really been concentrated on enough. It's very difficult for us to say how much can be achieved, but it's amazing, sometimes, what can be achieved through goodwill."

And the best goodwill Britain has to offer these days seems to be Princess Diana's image.

CAVEAT: Any attempt to calculate Di's economic value to Britain is, at best, doomed to wild inaccuracy and, at worst, frivolous. **ON THE OTHER HAND:** There's a time and place for frivolity. As the U.S. hunkers down for an unprecedented wave of Di-mentia, this is it.

WHAT'S DIANA WORTH TO BRITAIN?

- **THERE ARE, OF** course, any number of ways to calculate Di's value to Britain. For example, one could take the British Gross National Product, add the number of episodes in *Upstairs, Downstairs,* and divide the total by Di's shoe size (9½). A slightly more defensible number could be calculated by adding up the total sales of British products that have benefited through association with Di.

- **IN 1981 SHE WORE** a sweater decorated with cute little sheep (below); the manufacturer has now sold $1 million worth.

- **IN 1982 SHE MADE** flat shoes a fashion fad; one shoe company, Clarks, credits her with helping them sell 2.8 million pairs of shoes—or about $63 million worth. The list goes on:

- **A BRITISH PAPER-** back almanac, *The Book of Money Lists,* reports that 27 million copies of 112 different Di-inspired books have been sold. At, say, $5 per book, that comes to $135 million.

- **HER HAIRDRESSER** sold his story to a tabloid for a reported $140,000.

- **BROADCAST** and print rights to the couple's TV interview have brought an estimated $1.4 million, which will go to charity.

- **ADD IT ALL UP,** multiply the result by a factor of 3.3— because it's fun, and to account for unaccounted-for business—and credit Di with drumming up more than $650 million worth of commercial transactions.

- **WITH APOLOGIES** to Winston Churchill: Seldom, in the course of human endeavor, have so many owed so much to one officially unemployed mother of two.

A lightning rod for publicity, Princess Diana (donning a British Petroleum hard hat) plays a role both important and undefined.

Lind... ...ke you've never seen her before

OCTOBER 13, 1986 ■ $1.50

People weekly

FERGIE & DI

THE MERRY WIVES OF ● WINDSOR

NOW PLAYING AT THE PALACE

Fergie and Di, the best of friends and the toast of the town

"I T MUST BE daunting for her to come here and not know a soul," exclaimed a guest as the Duchess of York arrived alone for a charity dinner at London's Savoy Hotel two weeks ago. But within minutes the former Sarah Ferguson, swathed from cleavage to ankles in a shiny red-and-black satin ball gown, showed she was anything but overwhelmed. Sarah pranced around the room and greeted strangers as if they were old friends, laughed raucously at their jokes and even winked at admirers. At dinner, she consumed everything from fish mousse to strawberry soufflé with gusto, then, during a charity auction, exhorted bidders to pledge more money. "Come on, George, your wife wants it b-i-g!" she shouted to one startled participant.

By evening's end, the room was won over. Said lyricist Richard Stilgoe: "We always worry when a prince brings someone home—will she fit into the soap opera? Sarah has, very well."

Indeed. The newest member of the House of Windsor has become a wildly popular costar in the royal road show. In fact, if performances by members of the House of Windsor carried credits, Sarah, Duchess of York, would already be sharing top billing with Diana, Princess of Wales.

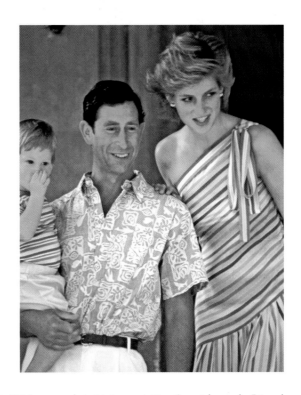

Even on holiday the Waleses work. In Majorca visiting Spanish royals, Di and Charles (with Prince Harry) posed for the press in between swimming and sailing.

Charles and Di faced off in Cannes last month. She wanted to stay; he wanted to fly home.

SOME FAIRY TALE. As Diana, the Princess of Wales, emerged from the London movie house where she had just seen Whoopi Goldberg's *Jumpin' Jack Flash,* she was spotted by six members of a West Indian street gang who had been loitering nearby. As she nervously made her way to her car, the gang moved toward her, pointing their fingers and shouting, "There she is!" Then, noticing that the princess's male escort wasn't the prince (he was, unbeknownst to them, Diana's bodyguard), one of the men began taunting her. "I'm gonna tell Charles," he warned. "I'm gonna tell Charles."

Well, let him. It's doubtful he could tell Charles anything that the future king—or anyone else in Britain—hasn't heard already.

HAPPILY? OR JUST EVER AFTER?

After six years a storybook marriage loses its glow

JUNE 8, 1987 ■ $1.50

People weekly

SAVE THE WALES!

She's coping, he's moping. After six years of marriage, CHARLES and DI have begun to lead separate lives

Space~~s~~ Brooks ● **The strange death of Althea Flynt**

JULY 20, 1987 ■ $1.69

People weekly

The follies of Fergie & Di

NAUGHTY, NAUGHTY

OCUS, IF YOU will, on
a few recent moments
ose wacky wives of
or. See Fergie, the
s of York, leaping into
n-law Diana's lap in the
ox at Ascot and refusing
dge herself until
s Anne drops by for a
e Diana giving Fergie
gles by standing up to
ten her clingy yellow
hen shaking the royal
ith the finesse of a
r. See Fergie and Di at
es, jabbing well-dressed
in the behinds with
mbrellas. Listen to Di
g snooty Princess
l of Kent: "Isn't that
s Michael?" she asks
with mock awe, within
t of their starchy
n-law.

After their brolly
folly at Ascot
last month, the
Sun newspaper
called the royal
buddies "silly,
simpering girls."

NO TITTERS, YOU TWO, THIS IS SERIOUS!

Cutting up royally, and nettled by a rumor of scandal,
those fun-loving Windsors Fergie and Di have worrywart
Britons wondering whither the stiff upper lip

APRIL 25, 1988 ■ $1.69

People weekly

Eleanor Mondale & her Bear:
The wedding album

GROWING UP ROYAL

How to raise an unspoiled, tiny monarch-in-waiting, in a world of ponies, palaces & miniature Jaguars

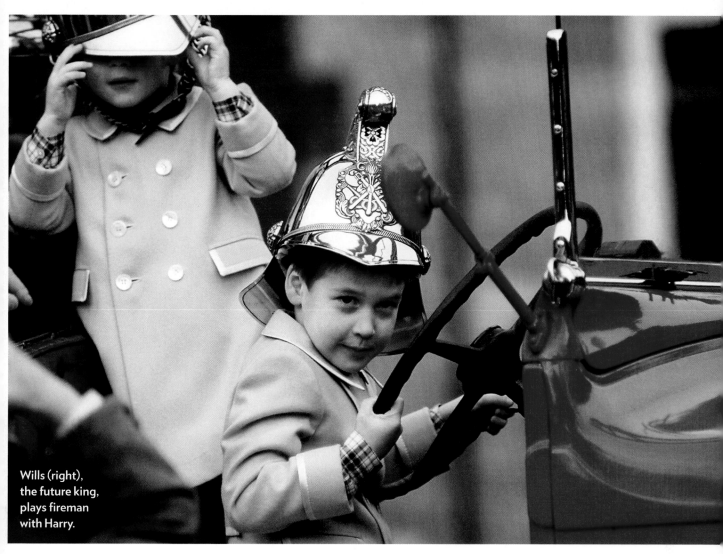

Wills (right),
the future king,
plays fireman
with Harry.

When it comes to raising England's privileged little princes, Princess Diana rules the roost

O
N A BLUSTERY day last January, Britain's Prince William, 5, clambered to the top of a red antique fire engine, clamped on an old-fashioned fireman's helmet, clanged the bell and exuberantly yelled, "Where's the fire?" The scene captured in microcosm the delights and drawbacks of perhaps the most extraordinary childhood in the world. For while many children dream of becoming firefighters when they grow up—and in the

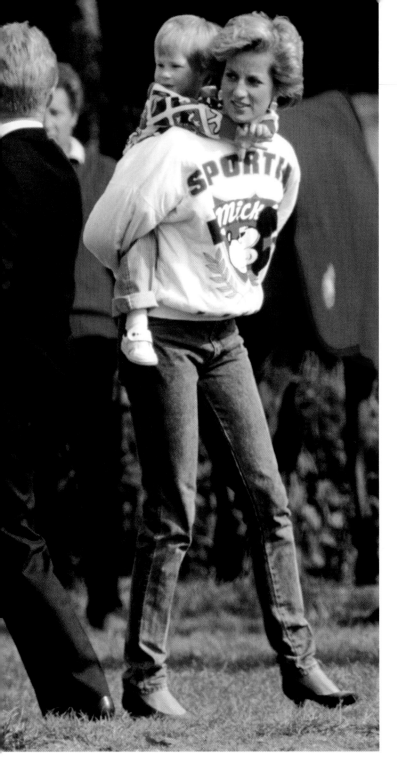

Wearing matching Mickey Mouse motifs, Diana and Harry frolicked last year. She clearly feels he needs extra coddling.

meantime would gladly settle for a rampage in a station house—the boy's play was a privileged but hardly spontaneous romp. Wills and his companions that day, younger brother Harry, 3, and cousins Peter and Zara Phillips (Princess Anne's children, 10 and 6, respectively), were clambering over a 1939 engine that once belonged to their great-grandfather King George VI. And they were on display at a pre-planned photo opportunity staged by Queen Elizabeth at her Sandringham estate in Norfolk for the benefit of a phalanx of photographers.

One day William will be swapping that aged helmet for an even rarer headpiece, the crown of the United Kingdom. That makes him one of the most curious creatures in the whole human zoo, the one whose difference from you and me isn't just a matter of money. What with palaces, toys galore and security guards, footmen and nannies at their every beck and call, the princes present their parents with the trickiest of tasks. It's up to Charles and Diana to master striking a balance between normality and nobility in the lives of the next generation of English royals.

Wills played Prince Charming to cousin Zara Phillips at this year's Easter services at Windsor. Catch his grown-up loafers!

Public scoldings are never fun, even for an experienced rascal like William. Here nanny Olga Powell takes Wills to task for acting up at one of Dad's polo matches.

Since 1986, the Waleses (above) have spent summer holidays in Majorca with Spain's Queen Sofia (right) and her family.

"I think he's absolutely miserable

—*Majesty* editor Ingrid Seward, on Charles

The invisible wedding of Michael J. Fox

AUGUST 1, 1988 ■ $1.69

People
weekly

SEVEN-YEAR HITCH

Happy Anniversary— or is it? Charles & Di and five U.S. couples who also got married this week in 1981 face that awful moment when marriage can feel like a bad dream

Thoug
polo fa
Diana
out Ch
a chuk
Winds
frenzy
leaves
(left, a
match

SEVEN YEAR HITCH

MORE OFTEN THAN not, it happens. In the course of marriage, a seven-year hitch is marked by the onset of the seven-year itch, a malady unknown to dermatologists but familiar to marriage counselors and victims of the disease. Symptoms: He stops holding the door and starts pointing to it; she stops making dinner and starts making reservations; he stops calling her dear and starts calling her expensive. Of course, when you're dealing with royalty, the symptoms of the itch take quite a different form: Perhaps she finds lipstick on his epaulet; maybe he notices that she leaves her tiaras lying around the palace and is relying more and more frequently on caviar helper at dinner. They fight about little things, like who's going to walk the polo ponies, and she's always yelling at him about why they have to spend so much time with his mother. He used to call her his little crown jewel; now he just wants to crown her.

OCTOBER 31, 1988 ■ $1.69

People weekly

Reaching 40, CHARLES builds a private LIFE WITHOUT DI

While he fishes, paints, broods over the symbols in his dreams & dallies abroad, Diana gets a taste of single motherhood

10227

0 724414 8

44

A DANGEROUS AGE

At 40 he is drifting away from Diana and his two sons into a separate life

Charles seemed to fall in love with Diana on their honeymoon; by their return to Balmoral in August 1981, he was besotted.

T'S JUST ANOTHER birthday," declared the Prince of Wales last week, but nobody has paid the slightest attention to his shy disclaimer. With two weeks to go before His Royal Highness hits the big four-O, England is preparing to honor the occasion in royal fashion. Bulging sacks of mail are arriving at the palace. A new biography of the prince, Alan

Charles (above, left, in 1957) has said his first days at Cheam School were "the most miserable of my life," but he adjusted.

Absurdly bewigged, Charles displayed theatrical flair as a Beatle in a 1968 Cambridge production of *Revolution*.

Hamilton's *The Real Charles,* has just been published, and an old one, Anthony Holden's *Prince Charles,* updated. ITV will air a special tribute to His Royal Highness, and on the day itself, Nov. 14, flags will fly on all public buildings, cannon will fire a 62-gun salute from the Tower of London, and bells will ring out all over the United Kingdom in honor of the man who (if he doesn't break his neck on a ski slope or a polo field) will one day be King.

Yet 40 is seldom the happiest of birthdays, even for a prince who surely has many a good reason to grin. Charles is the sole proprietor of estates totaling 131,744 acres that bring him an annual income of $2.8 million—not to mention 300 puffins a year from the Scilly Isles. When he ascends the throne he will also inherit a royal fortune worth better than $5 billion. He is married to Princess Diana, one of the world's most beautiful and fashionable women.

What more could a man want? Plenty, it would seem. As he enters what should be his most creative years, insiders say Charles is haunted by a sense that his per-

sonal life is meaningless and his princely role a glamorous sham. Some say Diana is now more interested in playing the superstar than she is in being a wife. Others think Charles is miffed because the press devotes pages to her wardrobe and inches to his ideas. One thing is horribly clear: The Waleses have almost nothing in common except their children—and their inability to communicate. And they seem to have stopped trying. In the past 10 months, Charles has gone on safari in Africa, fished for salmon in Iceland, hiked in the Hebrides, painted in Italy and rusticated in Balmoral—all without his family.

Even at home Charles is rarely around. He passes the day at his office-apartment in Buckingham Palace and often sleeps there too. On weekends he usually runs off to play polo. "Diana takes the boys to watch," says a friend, "because she knows that otherwise they won't get to see their dad."

Flanked by the Queen Mother and Princess Margaret for his mother's 1953 coronation, Prince Charles pensively eyed the pomp and circumstance that is his birthright.

"How is she ever… to be taken as anything more than an exquisitely coiffed airhead?

—Britain's *Sunday Times,* after a photographer caught Di swimming in a halter top

Vanna's court battle against a crazed ta...

JULY 16, 1990 ■ $1.95

People
weekly

THE WOMAN WHO WILL BE QUEEN

Ten years after she first caught Charles's eye, **PRINCESS DIANA** is nudging the royal family into the modern world. She drives the kids to school, does aerobics, reaches out to AIDS patients—and struggles to make a difficult marriage work

PRINCESS WITH A PURPOSE

OUR FIRST GLIMPSE of her will remain forever: a gawky 19-year-old kindergarten teacher balancing one child on a hip, holding the hand of another, gazing shyly at the camera. The image was of pure innocence—such innocence that she didn't even realize the sun was shining through her diaphanous skirt, giving the world an unexpectedly leggy view of the woman who will someday be Queen of England.

That September 1980 photo helped fire a fascination with Lady Diana Spencer, now the Princess of Wales, that has continued unabated. Even today, as she approaches the start of her second decade in our consciousness, she remains the most closely watched public beauty since Jacqueline Onassis. And like a hothouse flower, Diana has blossomed under the glare. The guileless girl in the schoolyard has become a seasoned royal performer who, with her elegant silk suits and wide-brimmed hats, not only looks the part, but lives it, forging an emotional connection with her countrymen that few other Windsors have achieved.

When Charles fell off his pony in June, Di didn't rush to his bedside—but she did retrieve him from the hospital (above).

Fund-raising Di took a sexy turn with the Royal Ballet's Wayne Sleep (far left) in 1985.

In 1980 an unpolished Di was caught with two charges in the Young England Kindergarten yard. Today, says one court observer, "she has star quality."

CAROLINE KENNEDY talks about her inspiring new book

FEBRUARY 11, 1991 ■ $1.95

People weekly

While **DIANA** puts on a brave face, a brooding **PRINCE CHARLES** grapples with a mid-life crisis and retreats to his old girlfriends

RICH, ROYAL AND . . .

HOME ALONE

10227 06

0 724414 8

T IS A rite of passage in many an upper-class household: seeing the children off to boarding school. And for the Prince and Princess of Wales, as for many others in Britain, it was enacted as a family. On Sept. 10 they glided in a Bentley up the drive of Ludgrove School, 25 miles west of London, with Prince William, 8, in tow. After meeting the headmaster and touring the dorm, Dad and Mom bid the lad adieu.

A touching scene of familial togetherness? Not exactly. The Bentley had whisked Charles from Highgrove, while Princess Diana had motored from London with Wills in her Jaguar. Only at the foot of the school drive was there a rendezvous, with Di and Wills climbing into the Bentley. After Wills was settled—and the family appearance had been recorded by photographers—Charles headed back to Highgrove and Di to Kensington Palace. That meeting—30 minutes in total—would mark the last time they would see each other for 39 days.

Wills kept pace with Mum on the way to his cousin Eugenie's christening (above).

"WINDOW PAIN" screamed a *Sun* headline when Charles was caught in this gloomy pose.

DI AND HER PRINCE: EVERYTHING BUT LOVE
Demoralized by a fall from a polo pony, Charles increasingly plays absentee husband

LEE R... ...od mourns a gallant beauty

JULY 22, 1991 $1.95

People

weekly

A DECADE LATER,

WHERE HAS THEIR LOVE GONE?

On its 10th anniversary, the storybook marriage of Charles and Diana is a painful fake. Now Britain openly asks the unthinkable: Is he fit to reign? Will they finally divorce?

ONCE UPON A TIME...

the world fell in love with a dashing prince and his enchanting bride. Ten years later Charles and Diana are not living happily ever after—and their troubled marriage may keep him from the throne

In an all-too-familiar scenario —where is Dad?— a most maternal Diana posed with Wills and Harry at Highgrove.

THE EUPHORIA WAS overwhelming, the images unforgettable. PERFECT! proclaimed Britain's *Daily Mail* in the banner headline over its front-page photo of the kissing newlyweds. THE VERY PICTURE OF FAIRY-TALE SWEETHEARTS, echoed the *Sun*. It was July 29, 1981, the wedding of His Royal Highness the Prince of Wales and Lady Diana Spencer,

Preferring solitary pursuits, Charles retreated on Easter Sunday, 1989, to sketch in the grounds of Windsor Castle.

The flame has flickered for nearly 20 years between Charles and his sometime hostess, Camilla Parker Bowles, 43 (shown tanking up last May).

seemingly destined to become King and Queen of England. Tens of millions of Americans set their alarms for before dawn to watch the live telecast, which had a worldwide audience of 750 million. It was all spectacle and wonderment and celebration, not a day to doubt. Thus few pondered the point made by the officiating Archbishop of Canterbury, Dr. Robert Runcie, about a wedding day being not "the place of arrival, but the place where the adventure really begins." Nobody, least of all an adoring British public, wanted to believe this marriage could go wrong. But it has. If only as a sop to the masses, some royalty watchers anticipated a demonstration of togetherness on Di's 30th birthday on July 1. It was not to be. According to some reports, Charles offered to throw her a party, but Di declined, celebrating instead with friends in London while he remained at their country house, Highgrove. Today, faced with such evidence, it is hard for even the most blinkered royalist to claim that Charles and Diana's marital adventure is other than a pretense, sustained only because of the messy constitutional problems that would arise from a formal separation or divorce.

With Charles
absent, Di and
Wills rooted
Steffi Graf
on to her
Wimbledon title.

"When it counts, we stand together

—Diana to a friend on her and her siblings'
strained relationship with their stepmother

IVANA'S REVENGE: New book & an Italian lover. (*Ciao*, Donald)

APRIL 13, 1992 $1.99

People
weekly

DIANA IN MOURNING

A difficult month comes to a tragic end as the Princess of Wales copes with the sudden death of her father

I T WAS A rare scene of Wales family togetherness: Princess Diana, in a white robe and wet hair, standing on a hotel balcony in Austria and cheering on Prince Charles and their two young sons in a snowball fight below. But after a month of family woes focused on the marital breakup of her brother-in-law Andrew and the Duchess of York, Di would find her own happiness suddenly undone as well. Abruptly called to the phone, the princess learned that her father, the 68-year-old eighth Earl Spencer, had died unexpectedly of a heart attack in London. Returning to the balcony, visibly shaken, Diana pleaded with nearby photographers to "please, just leave us alone" and called her family together. Later that night a black dress—royals customarily pack mourning attire when they travel—was seen being aired outside their suite.

Princess Diana struggles with the sudden death of the father she loved

A SPECIAL

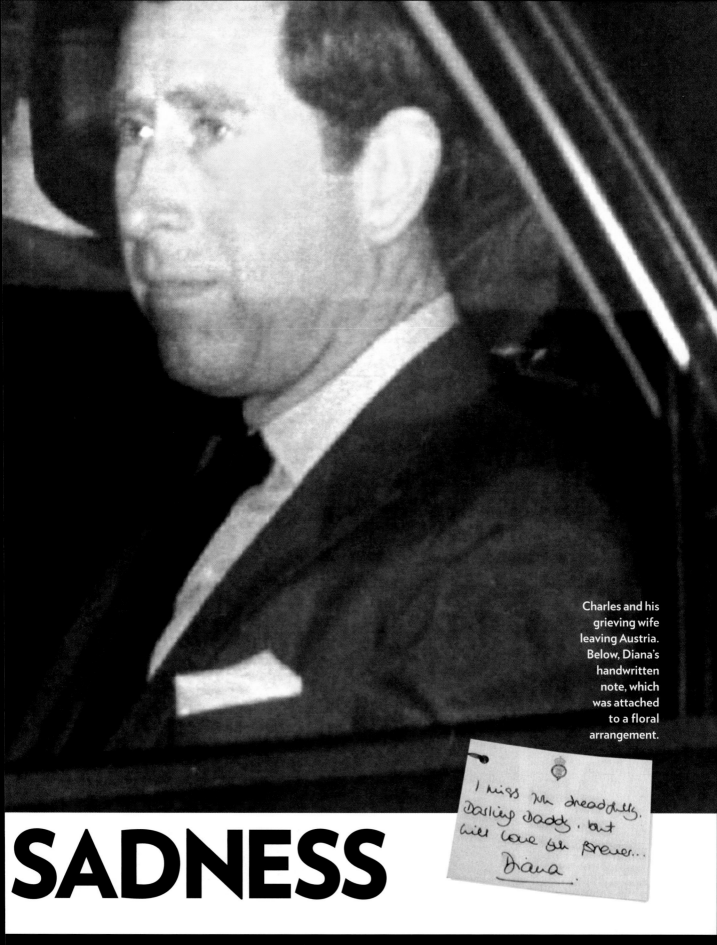

Charles and his grieving wife leaving Austria. Below, Diana's handwritten note, which was attached to a floral arrangement.

I miss you dreadfully, Darling Daddy, but will love you forever... Diana.

SADNESS

PART FOUR

THINGS FALL APART

JUNE 22, 1992 $1.99

People

weekly

DIANA

DRAMATIC EXCERPTS FROM THE BOOK THAT ROCKED BRITAIN

PLUS: TOUCHING PHOTOS FROM DI'S FAMILY ALBUM

A GRIM FAIRY TALE

A startlingly candid new biography of Diana tracks the troubled life of the woman who would be Queen

When the prince, then 32, proposed to the 19-year-old teacher in 1981 (above), Diana still called him Sir.

BEHIND THE PUBLIC smiles, Princess Diana is a lonely and unhappy young woman who endures a loveless marriage," writes Andrew Morton in his explosive biography *Diana: Her True Story,* which is currently rattling the Wedgwood at Buckingham Palace. Following an excerpt published in London's *Sunday Times* last weekend, the Queen reportedly summoned Charles for a crisis conference, the Archbishop of Canterbury publicly clucked over the pushy press, and the

famed Harrods banned the book.

Morton, 38, says he had cooperation from Diana's friends, family and counselors. Though the Palace isssued a statement asserting that the princess had not granted any interviews to the author, there has been no denial of the revelations. Following are excerpts:

• *After discovering, days before her wedding, that Charles was involved with Camilla Parker Bowles, Diana told her sisters she was thinking of calling off the marriage.*

"Bad luck, Duch," they said, using the family nickname, "Duchess," for their younger sister. "Your face is on the tea towels, so it's too late to chicken out now. . . ."

• On her first New Year within the royal family, Diana threatened to take her own life. Charles accused her of crying wolf and prepared to go riding. She hurled herself down a staircase, falling in a heap at the first landing. . . . During a heated argument with Prince Charles, she picked up a penknife and cut her chest and her thighs. Although she was bleeding, her husband scorned her. As ever, he thought she was faking her problems. . . .

• Diana lived on an emotional see-saw, her jealousy matched by a sublime devotion to Charles. . . .

DIANA AS A CHILD

By the time she was 6, Diana Spencer (above, at age 2) had been devastated by the breakup of her parents' marriage. From age 9 onward she attended boarding schools (below); at West Heath in Kent, which her sisters also attended, the youngest Spencer is remembered as chubby and bashful. Apparently her affinity for hats started early (right).

"I always felt very detached from everyone else," Diana (striking a pose, above) has said of her childhood. "I knew I was going somewhere different."

The future Princess of Wales takes a flying leap from the family waterslide (above, right). The red dots on her suit are swimming badges.

Di poses at age 10 with Riddlesworth Hall classmates (right), all of whom no doubt later remarked, at least once in their lives, "You're kidding! That quiet little blonde girl from fifth grade?!?!?"

"Why don't you leave my husband alone?

—Diana to Camilla at a 1984 party

A TEENAGE 'FATAL ATTRACTION' CASE

JUNE 29, 1992 $1.99

People

weekly

BATMAN BASH

JUNE 29 1992

THE OTHER WOMAN
DIANA'S RIVAL

Diana in tears

Camilla at a polo match

For two decades Charles has sought comfort and companionship with a married woman. Now his bond with Camilla Parker Bowles could cost him the throne.

LOVE ON THE ROCKS

A furor thrusts Camilla Parker Bowles, Prince Charles's longtime companion, center stage

THE WOMAN WHO darkened Di's life is a wife and mother who is happiest "hunting for grouse in a howling wind," in the words of one friend. Camilla Parker Bowles has none of Princess Diana's coltish elegance. A jodhpurs-and-wellies sort whose hair usually looks as if she's spent the day on a damp racecourse, she has a figure that is no longer girlish, and her crow's-feet reflect character more than camouflage. Indeed, there is the air about her of a woman too busy to trifle with facials, manicures or lace-trimmed teddies.

Yet unlikely as it may seem, Parker Bowles has been cast as a lead in the drama that has rocked the House of Windsor and could cost Prince Charles, 43, the throne. Described by friends as his longtime "confidante," she was a prominent character in Andrew Morton's sensational *Diana: Her True Story,* the biography (excerpted in PEOPLE June 22) in which the Waleses' marriage was portrayed as a loveless misalliance between a volatile depressive and a selfish twit. In recent weeks British tabloids have served up stories describing the princess's jealousy of Camilla and dissected the rivalry between the two women. Diana, Morton reports, calls Charles's companion "the Rottweiler," while Camilla reportedly refers to the princess as "that ridiculous creature."

Camilla Parker Bowles (left) at a June 6 polo match. The prince, says an insider, believes Di cooperated with the Andrew Morton book and is "spitting bricks over her betrayal." Diana (right) burst into tears after a visit to a hospice on June 11.

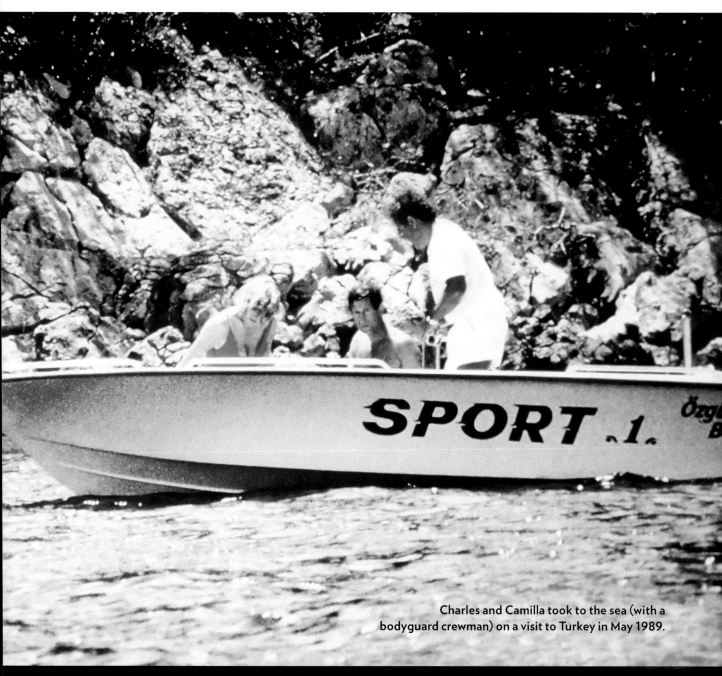

Charles and Camilla took to the sea (with a bodyguard crewman) on a visit to Turkey in May 1989.

AN ALL ——— OUT FOR WHITNEY'S WEDDING

Whitney Houston and husband Bobby Brown

AUGUST 3, 1992 $1.99

People
weekly

BATTLING BULIMIA

DIANA'S DIET ORDEAL

How the stress of royal life plunged Di into a secret struggle with the dangerous binge-and-purge eating disorder that affects millions of young women

The thin Princess in 1989.

"I think . . . the whole thing was triggered during her honeymoon when her husband put his arms around her and said, 'You are a bit chubby, darling'

—*Diana: Her True Story* author Andrew Morton

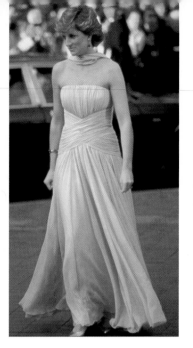

In 1981, says Campbell, the newly engaged Diana (far left), 19, felt she looked too "matronly."

By 1982, Diana had grown so thin that palace watchers whispered she had anorexia (center).

Different day, different Di: By 1987, the princess again presented a more well-rounded figure (right).

The princess's struggle with bulimia brings a puzzling disease out of the shadows

DI'S PRIVATE BATTLE

O N HER HONEYMOON she raided the galley of the royal yacht *Britannia* for ice cream. At Windsor Castle a footman caught her scarfing down an entire steak-and-kidney pie. During an evening of bridge, friends saw her devour a pound of candy. And at a 1989 charity dinner in Manhattan, a guest watched with alarm while Princess Diana "hunched over her food and shoveled it in, broke the roll with her teeth and used her finger for a pusher. It was astonishing." Hardly what one would expect from a lithe specimen like the Princess of Wales—who, at 5'10", weighs in at about 127 lbs. But while she may have a humongous appetite, Diana, 31, has weathered two pregnancies, countless state dinners and 11 demanding years in the spotlight while keeping herself trim—and, at times, even gaunt. Her secret, as revealed this summer with the publication of a trio of bestselling biographies, is not a pretty one. Though only Diana and the therapists who reportedly have treated her know for sure, the princess is believed to have suffered from bulimia nervosa— the binge-and-purge syndrome that afflicts millions of American women.

Diana (in Canada in 1991) "has always had a monumental appetite," says biographer Lady Colin Campbell.

**"Squidge,
cover them footsteps!**

—James Gilbey, in an infamous taped phone call,
laughingly encouraging Princess Diana ("Squidge")
to keep their upcoming rendezvous secret

Murphy Brown's real nemesis: her boss, M

SEPTEMBER 14, 1992 $1.99

People

weekly

Candice Bergen & Grant Shaud

DIANA'S SECRETS

The furor over the tape, the tattletale, and two men too close to Di

Below: Diana's intimate friend James Gilbey; at left, her riding instructor, Major James Hewitt

"Bloody hell," Diana complains about the Windsors during taped calls to Gilbey (on the run from paparazzi), "after all I've done for this f------ family."

FOR CYNICS WHO savor tales of domestic chaos chez Windsor, it was the decade's most delicious scandalfest: No sooner had British tabloids splayed photos of a topless Duchess of York across their lurid pages than it was her sister-in-law's turn to take the heat. On Aug. 24 the transcript of a 23-minute phone conversation between the Princess of Wales and close friend James Gilbey was published in *The Sun,* revealing to the world that 1) she answers to the nickname Squidgy; 2) she describes life with Prince Charles as "real torture"; and 3) she sometimes catches the 92-year-old Queen Mum watching her "with a strange look in her eyes." The tape's chummy dialogue (the word "darling" pops up more than 20 times) quickly touched off a round of speculation about the princess's friendships with bachelors like Gilbey, a well-born man-about-town whom she has known since 1979. But the conversation also exposed a side of Di that the bedazzled British public often ignores: With its giggly chatter about shopping, spending and horoscopes, the transcript made her sound like a dim-bulb Sloane Ranger surrounded by sycophants. In the words of John Casey, Fellow of Gonville and Caius College, Cambridge, who lambasted Di and her "moronic friends" in the *Evening Standard,* "The princess comes across as a birdbrained egomaniac."

DIANA UNDER FIRE

In the latest installment from the battered House of Windsor, a kissy-kissy tape and a witness's tale of an intimate rendezvous put Di on the hot seat

A former lance corporal said he had witnessed decidedly indiscreet action between the princess and her riding instructor Maj. James Hewitt (receiving a polo trophy from Diana in Wiltshire in 1991).

"I simply can't face the farce of a happy family Christmas

—Diana, to friends

Denzel Washington and the real MALCOLM X

NOVEMBER 30, 1992 $1.99

People weekly

IT'S OVER

10227

0 724414 8

48

GOING IT ALONE

He loves another woman.
She has given up the sham.
Now Buckingham Palace faces
the inevitable—a split decision

IN THE ONGOING soap opera that passes for the marriage of the Prince and Princess of Wales, even veteran royal-watchers have had trouble at times separating substance from suds. This month, though, all the rumor, rancor and behind-the-scenes maneuvering surrounding the royal couple finally reached a denouement. Except for the sounding

At a ceremony in South Korea, Charles and Diana "were inches apart . . . but it might have been miles," noted one observer. In four days their eyes barely met.

The Waleses agree on one thing: Harry (left) and Wills (at a London museum in April) will remain in Diana's charge and the family's good graces.

Camilla Parker Bowles (with Charles at Balmoral in 1990) has what a friend of her husband's has called "an open and free" marriage.

of taps and the reading of the scroll, the marriage is—for just about all practical purposes—over.

The last scrap of official pretense was swept away after two weeks of headline events: a disastrous joint trip abroad; a startling statement from Di reflecting her marital woes; and, finally, reports of a new love tape, this one starring Charles and his euphemistically described "confidante," Camilla Parker Bowles, 45. By mid-month, British papers were reporting that Charles was thinking about pulling out of the whole sticky mess and handing over his place in line to the throne to his son William, 10. (Wills, meanwhile, showing a dearth of royal dignity himself, had just been knuckle-rapped at school for trying to flush a schoolmate's head down the toilet.)

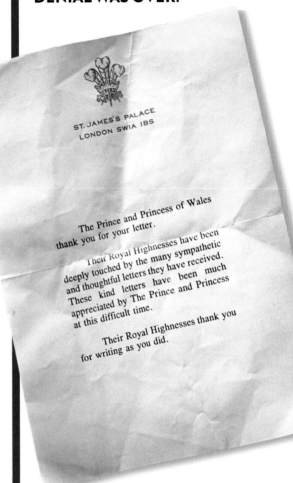

ST. JAMES'S PALACE
LONDON SW1A 1BS

The Prince and Princess of Wales thank you for your letter.

Their Royal Highnesses have been deeply touched by the many sympathetic and thoughtful letters they have received. These kind letters have been much appreciated by The Prince and Princess at this difficult time.

Their Royal Highnesses thank you for writing as you did.

THE QUEEN'S POSITION

At the urging of Robert Fellowes, the Queen's private secretary and Diana's brother-in-law, the princess issued a statement that described Elizabeth II as "sympathetic and supportive" to Di as she and Charles, living apart, contemplate formalizing the arrangement.

"**A phoenix princess [will arise] from the ashes of this whole crumbling mess of a monarchy**

—author and Diana confidant Andrew Morton

The good news for the Windsors: Annie gets her gr[o]

Princess Anne

DECEMBER 21, 1992 $1.99

People weekly

DIANA MAKES A DEAL

Separated from Prince Charles, she gets what she wants: palace digs, co-custody of the kids and a chance to be queen

SEPARATE

In a light moment in 1986, Diana bashed Charles with a prop champagne bottle—
but more serious cracks were already showing.

After years of misery, the parting's over, and Charles and Di look to the future

LIVES

S HISTORIC ANNOUNCEMENTS go, it was hardly a shocker: For months, palace watchers had predicted the Prince and Princess of Wales would abandon their desperately unhappy marriage. The only question was whether the savvy Diana would manage to keep the symbols of power—and the dignity—that the Duchess of York left behind when she said goodbye to Prince Andrew.

When British Prime Minister John Major broke the news of the royal separation to the House of Commons at 3:30 p.m. on Dec. 9, it became clear the princess had prevailed. Reading from a statement issued by the Palace, Major announced that the Waleses, "with regret," had decided to separate, although there were no plans for a divorce. "This decision has been reached amicably," read the dispatch, "and they will both continue to participate fully in the upbringing of their children." In his own statement, Major added that "there is no reason why the Princess of Wales should not be crowned Queen in due course."

AN INDEPENDENT WOMAN

Oscar ... es! Tresses! Bizarre Excesses!

APRIL 12, 1993 $2.29

People
weekly

Winner Marisa Tomei,
in Chanel

DIANA ON HER OWN

The perils—and pleasures—of life without Charles

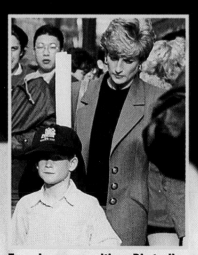

Forgoing pomp, citizen Di strolls
a London street with Harry, 8

10227

0 724414 8

15

"**The people with power are rallying behind the prince, and she is feeling the backlash**

—a friend of Di's

"The downgrading was definitely on Palace orders," one observer said of Diana's five-day visit to Nepal, where she was not afforded the royal treatment she enjoyed on earlier visits. "It was a subtle way of trying to put her in her place."

From flying business class to a semi-snub
in Kathmandu, the Princess of Wales
copes with life after Charles

DI GOES IT ALONE

WHEN LADY DIANA Spencer
walked into St. Paul's Cathedral
on her wedding day in 1981, her future seemed
as set and unswerving as the flower-bedecked
aisle before her. Stepping into a role defined by
tradition and bound by ritual, the Princess of
Wales was expected to do as her predecessors
had done—stand by her man, produce an heir
and a spare and help preserve the mystique of
the monarchy. Now, 12 years later, Diana's path looks more like a minefield,
and the principal constants in her life are its contradictions.

During his own
recent jaunts to
Croatia and to
Mexico (where
he communed
with cacti in
Oaxaca), Charles
acted like the
unfettered
Action Prince
of old.

Since her separation from Prince Charles she has gained a measure of pre-
cious freedom, but hardly enough to seek other loves and liaisons. Although
distanced from the royal family, she is raising a son who will one day be King.
And though the British public still prefers her to Charles, she is seen by some
as a deserter—a renegade who, without the Palace to smooth the way, is vul-
nerable to the sort of embarrassments endured by mere celebrities. Just a
year ago, the current situation would have been unthinkable: cartoons of a
seminude Diana splayed across the pages of a British tabloid; broadcast
excerpts from a phone chat in which she and confidant James Gilbey dis-
cussed her fear of getting pregnant; an awkward visit to Nepal, where
Buckingham Palace apparently asked her hosts to down-scale her welcome.

"You make my life hell!

—Diana to a photographer in Leicester Square

Michael Jackson fights child abuse

SEPTEMBER 6, 1993 $2.29

People
weekly

The Fugitive's
Tommy Lee Jones

DIANA VS. CHARLES
BATTLE FOR THE BOYS

Diana, Harry
(center) and Wills
last April at a
theme park near
London

Royal pawns in a tense family rivalry, Wills, 11, and Harry, 8, frolicked at the Magic Kingdom as the tug-of-war between their parents escalated. Here is how the split has changed the little princes' lives

PING-PONG PRINCES

Bouncing back and forth between Di and Charles, William and brother Harry deal with the stresses of living in two different worlds

CYNICS CALLED IT the boldest gesture ever made by the image-conscious Princess Diana: On Aug. 24 she swept Prince William, 11, and Prince Harry, 8, off to Florida to begin a 10-day vacation guaranteed to attract every newshound in North America. With Fleet Street camped out in Orlando, she would have the opportunity not only to take her sons on an unforgettable outing to Disney World but also to demonstrate that she—and not Prince Charles—was the boys' more dedicated

Close friends, Harry (left) and William share a peaceful
moment in London's Kensington Gardens in July.

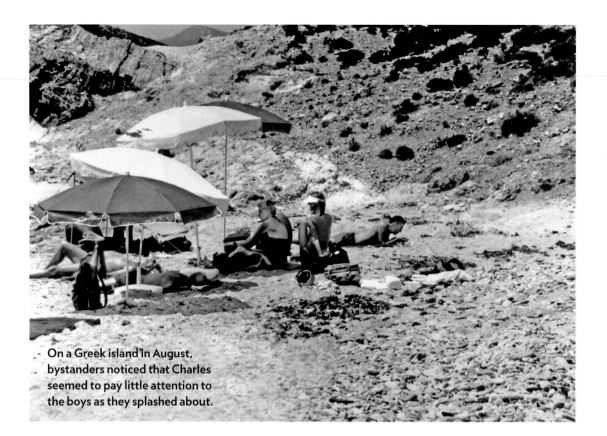

On a Greek island in August, bystanders noticed that Charles seemed to pay little attention to the boys as they splashed about.

parent. Two hours after their British Airways flight landed in Orlando at 3 p.m., Diana and her party were shrieking down Splash Mountain, which reportedly had been closed to other visitors. Accompanied by close friends Kate Menzies, 32, and Catherine Soames, 35, plus Soames's son Harry, 9, and three detectives, Diana and the boys hit Big Thunder Mountain Railroad and took the Jungle Cruise before returning to the pricey Grand Floridian hotel. The next day, the group was spotted at the Disney-MGM Studios Theme Park, where they thrilled to the Indiana Jones Epic Stunt Spectacular.

Casting for trout with his kilted father at Balmoral in August, Harry enjoyed the outing.

Just the week before, Di's estranged husband had scored his own coup. On holiday with his sons at Balmoral, Charles, who normally shuns photo ops, made a valiant attempt to counteract his image as a distant father by allowing an ITV crew to shoot him fishing with his sons on the banks of Scotland's Loch Muick. Nine months after their parents' separation, Princes William and Harry are in the midst of a royal public relations tug-of-war.

Harry and William (right) helped Charles at a polo match in Windsor Great Park last spring.

"A divorce would drive her into oblivion, and she knows it

—Brian Hoey, royal author

SURPRISE! LUKE PERRY TAKES A BRIDE

DECEMBER 6, 1993 $2.29

People
weekly

LUKE & MINNIE

A YEAR AFTER THE SEPARATION

DIANA'S LONELY BATTLE

As the pros at the Palace squeeze her out, the isolated Princess jokes publicly about her mental health—and staying home with her 'head down the loo'

49

10227

0 724414 8

Lonely and
embattled,
Princess Diana
is learning some
hard lessons
about life without
Charles—and is
showing signs of
cracking under
the strain

THE OUTSIDER

BY ANY RECKONING it had been a difficult week for the Princess of Wales. On Nov. 1, Diana turned up 10 minutes late for a charity gala at London's Equinox Disco-Tec, wearing a lacy, high-on-the-thigh ensemble that seemed a tad outré. Pale and agitated, she "appeared to have used a lot of eyeliner to cover up tears," in the words of one witness. Midway through the performance, a detective escorted the teary princess out a back door and rushed her home to Kensington Palace. (The official explanation: a migraine.) The next day brought further distress. At a memorial service for the Earl of Westmorland, Diana found herself in the company of Prince Charles's longtime confidante Camilla Parker Bowles. As Di took her place in a pew in the Guards Chapel, Wellington Barracks, "Charles's mistress kept her eyes fixed on the floor," *Today* newspaper reported. Though the archrivals ignored one another, few were unaware of their discomfort.

To avoid an awkward encounter between Charles and Di, the Palace sent the princess to Northern Ireland for Remembrance Sunday, Nov. 14, while the other Windsors attended a service in London

GETTING BURNED

DI WAS STEAMED AFTER SHOTS OF HER IN A GYM HIT THE STREET
In the words of the London *Sunday Mirror*, the graphic shots featured in its Nov. 7 edition represented "the Princess of Wales as you have never seen her." Indeed. Lying on a machine ironically known as the Throne, a trim Diana was shown in leotard and cycling shorts with her shapely legs braced in an unregal pose that would have given Queen Victoria the vapors.

...is affair on the set cost millions?

JUNE 13, 1994 $2.39

People

weekly

DIANA'S DARING NEW LIFE

**Topless bathing?
Holistic healing?
Aromatherapy?
Anything goes,
as a liberated
Diana struggles
to find herself**

`0 72440 10227 9` 24

TAKING THE HEAT

Bored and unhappy, Di's adrift with the press in pursuit

Lensmen snapped controversial pictures of Di while she was in Spain, but some of the more risqué shots were never published.

FOR A WOMAN once revered by the British press, it was a distressing month indeed. On May 1, a photographer surreptitiously snapped the Princess of Wales lounging bare-breasted on the Costa del Sol, and (ignoring the fact that she had pleaded for privacy last December) Fleet Street

began wondering how the mother of a future king could have landed in such a scrape. Two weeks later, the tabloids were throbbing with an unflattering tale planted by Prince Charles's pals, who let reporters know that Diana had lavished $240,000 on personal expenses, including such minor items as manicures and supplies of Evian water, in the year that ended in March.

Never one to let her enemies have the last slur, Di fought back: One

day after the spending story broke, a leak to the *Daily Mail* led to a front-page exclusive about the princess helping to rescue a tramp who had nearly drowned in a Regent's Park lake. On the same day, the press got hold of details about Charles's finances and reported that the tab for his own indulgences (including six Savile Row suits and an Aston Martin) was a dizzying $650,000—$410,000 more than his estranged wife had spent.

At Daphne's restaurant in April, Di had a kiss for pal William von Straubenzee and an angry gesture for a photographer.

The l... ...love with TV's Lauren Holly

•SEPTEMBER 5 1994•

SEPTEMBER 5, 1994 $2.39

People

weekly

DIANA ON THE EDGE

The true story behind those phantom phone calls that have friends and family questioning her stability

0 72440 10227 9

36

A PRINCESS IN PERIL

FOR TWO WEEKS, it looked as if the Princess of Wales had reclaimed the privacy she says she craves: During her idyll on Martha's Vineyard, Mass., early last month, she managed to relax with close chum Lucia Flecha de Lima (wife of Brazil's ambassador to the U.S.) in a secluded manor house. Discreet residents kept Di sightings to themselves, and her social secrets were well-kept.

Three days after she returned to London, however, Diana, 33, was dealt a humiliating blow. In a story headlined "Di's Cranky Phone Calls to Married Tycoon," the tabloid *News of the World*

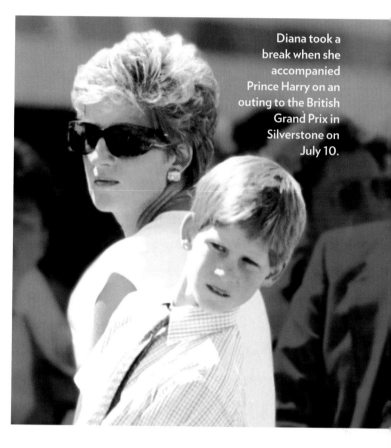

Diana took a break when she accompanied Prince Harry on an outing to the British Grand Prix in Silverstone on July 10.

claimed that over a period of 18 months the princess had made as many as 300 anonymous calls to platonic confidant Oliver Hoare. As the tabloid told it, the lonely, obsessive Di had rung his $3.5 million home in Chelsea as often as five times a day.

The explosive story raised several troubling points—the most provocative of which involved Di's state of mind. For some time both friends and enemies have wondered whether the embattled princess is on the verge of a breakdown. Since 1992, when Andrew Morton, author of *Diana: Her True Story*, revealed that she suffered from bulimia and had made several cry-for-help suicide attempts, insiders have spoken more freely about her mental problems. As one veteran Di watcher has put it, "She's all over the place and probably heading for a complete breakdown."

Accused of harassing a married friend with silent phone calls, a troubled Diana seems to be spinning out of control

OBER 17, 1994 $2.39

People
weekly

DIANA'S SECRET LOVER

Capt. James Hewitt's tattle-tale of love, lust and tears may earn millions—but how badly has his betrayal damaged Diana?

PLUS: Excerpts from the book that rocked Britain

The lady's chatty lover

> **"It is making the royal family a worldwide laughingstock**
>
> —a member of the Queen's Privy Council

DISS AND TELL

An ex-officer, but no gentleman, James Hewitt steps forth, breathes heavily and cashes in on his nearly five-year romance with a seductive Di

IN MANY WAYS, it sounds like nothing so much as a Barbara Cartland bodice ripper. The erotically charged story of a doomed affair between a future queen and a dashing officer, *Princess in Love* is the kind of book whose protagonists "feel as though their splintered souls had . . . become one."

Ironic, then, that all England is in a lather over the tawdry "memoir," a collaboration between journalist Anna Pasternak and ex-Life Guards officer James Hewitt, 36, who claims to have been Princess Diana's lover from 1986 until 1991. Rumors had been circulating for years. When *Princess in Love* was published Oct. 3, readers didn't stop to ask whether he was dishing up something new. Inspired by leaks in the London press that Di's lover was telling all, Britons rushed to bookstores; by lunchtime the first run of 75,000 was sold out.

Di was said to be "hurt and bitterly disappointed" by the Hewitt book.

In 1990, Di was caught in a kiss with Hewitt, then her riding instructor, near Windsor (above).

"I suppose it could quite easily be seen that I am a cad," Hewitt (left, playing the country squire in his mother's barn) has conceded.

Audre[...] [...]d lover share their memories

OCTOBER 31, 1994 $2.39

People

weekly

HE NEVER LOVED HER

Charles' shocking confession makes divorce certain—and leaves Britain wondering if he is fit to be King

Inside: Exclusive Excerpt

0 72440 10227 9

44

PRINCE OF PIQUE

Bidding for sympathy, Charles slams his wife and parents—and, perhaps, shoots himself in the foot

BY ANY RECKONING, it was an enormous gamble. Struggling with his image as the diffident twit who sabotaged his fairy-tale marriage, the Prince of Wales decided to abandon his decorous silence. Apparently hoping to convince his prospective subjects that he is a conscientious soul worthy to wear the crown, Prince Charles, 45, in a documentary aired last June, shocked the nation by confirming rumors he had committed adultery, but that was only the beginning. In author Jonathan Dimbleby's astonishingly candid new book, *The Prince of Wales: A Biography*, the prince is portrayed as an emotionally deprived pawn abandoned by his mother, bullied by his father and tortured by a paranoid wife whom he may never have loved. As he put it in a 1986 diary entry quoted in the book, "Frequently I feel . . . that I'm in a kind of cage, pacing up and down and longing to be free."

Unfortunately the notoriously impolitic Charles badly misjudged the British public. His apologia has been received with contempt. Accusing Charles of betraying the Queen, Princess Diana and his sons, the newspaper *Today* noted, "The book reveals a self-obsessed, self-indulgent and selfish man constantly turning molehills of problems into insurmountable mountains. . . . There must now be serious doubt about his fitness to wear the Crown."

Lord Mountbatten (in 1977) counseled his great-nephew (above) to avoid the kind of entanglements that forced Edward VIII's "disgraceful abdication."

SELENA VERDICT: HER FATHER SPEAKS OUT

NOVEMBER 6, 1995

People
weekly

**Marcia Clark and
Chris Darden: Just pals**

ROYAL ROULETTE
DIANA &
CAMILLA

As Charles parties in
public with his mistress,
a stronger, sexier Diana
returns to the royal
spotlight to fight her
homewrecker image

Charles and Camilla, socializing openly in London on October 18

$2.49

45

10227

0 724414 8

GOING PUBLIC

As Diana tries to rehab a smirched reputation, Charles steps out with the woman he loves

Di wore Lacroix to display her newly athletic figure during a September visit to Le Petit Palais in Paris.

JUST DAYS BEFORE, Palace watchers had been buzzing about the latest volley between the Princess of Wales and her putative rival Julia Carling. The *Daily Mail* reported on Oct. 11 that, furious at being branded "a homewrecker" because of her friendship with rugby star Will Carling (who separated from Julia in September), Di had wondered whether to suggest a tête-à-tête with his estranged wife "to clear the air." According to the *Mail,* the notion was rejected, and she complained about "being used" by Ms. Carling. Days later, on cue, the tabloid *News of the World* reported that Julia had cried on the shoulder of hairdresser Daniel

Diana went for a daring halter look and flirty slit skirt by Catherine Walker at a dinner for London's Serpentine Gallery on June 28.

On Sept. 7, Di stole the show at the London premiere of *Apollo 13* (where she met Tom Hanks) in a short $3,750 Versace sheath. "Diana the Huntress!" screamed the *Evening Standard*.

For a Sept. 12 soirée in Modena, Italy, Di made a splash in a shorter, white version of the Versace number she'd worn in London.

DI STRUTS HER (PUMPED-UP) STUFF

She began the year in sensible, knee-length suits, but lately Diana has favored short skirts and daring neck-lines—the better, perhaps, to show off the quads and biceps the iron-pumping princess brings home from the gym. Reviews from fashion mavens have been mixed. While some love the new look, the *Daily Express* dismissed the bolder Di as "a vamp."

Galvin Jr., "I can't compete with a princess."

Then, on Oct. 18, Di's most formidable rival, the freshly divorced Camilla Parker Bowles, eclipsed the sniping. That evening, Camilla attended a high-profile party at which Charles made an astonishing appearance. Showing off her slightly trimmed-down figure in a boldly décolleté black gown, a radiant, blonder Camilla beamed at photographers as she swept into London's Ritz Hotel. To the amazement of the paparazzi, the prince strolled past 90 minutes later on his way to the same fete. When Fleet Street seized the story, it was Camilla—not Diana—who was portrayed as the predator who snared a married man.

"There were three of us in this marriage, so it was a bit crowded

—Diana, describing how in 1985 her "woman's instinct" led her to suspect Charles was seeing Camilla Parker Bowles

BLOOD LUST: Seducer or serial killer?

DECEMBER 4, 1995

People
weekly

Smooth talker Glen Rogers is accused of killing four women

DIANA'S REVENGE
TAKE THAT!

$2.49

49
10227
0 724414 8

❝ I'll fight to the end, because I believe that I have a role to fulfill, and I've got two children to bring up

—Diana to Martin Bashir, about her intention to continue battling what she claimed were efforts by Prince Charles's aides to marginalize her

TRUE CONFESSIONS

Defying the Palace, a calculating Princess Diana takes the offensive in the battle for Britain's sympathies and admits to an affair of her own

T O SOME, IT seemed a spectacularly self-destructive act—one that plunged the monarchy into "the greatest crisis since the Abdication," in the words of London's *Daily Mail*. Three years after allowing journalist Andrew Morton to document her misery in a bestselling biography, and 18 months after Prince Charles retaliated by suggesting in a TV interview that he had been unfaithful, the Princess of Wales revived her devastating public relations battle with her husband. In a startlingly frank interview with the BBC's Martin Bashir on the Nov. 20 edition of its critically acclaimed news show *Panorama,* a strained-looking Di, 34, parried Charles's confession by acknowledging that she had had an affair with former Life Guards officer James Hewitt, 37, whom she said she had "adored." Portraying herself as an innocent struggling to cope with a voracious press, vindictive courtiers and a self-involved husband, the princess declared that, as unhappy as her marriage may be, she has no desire to end it. That move, she says, will be up to Charles—who, it seems, must now choose between appearing to be a cad or a coward. Watched by more than 21.5 million people in Britain and expected to draw millions more during an ABC News *Turning Point* special on Nov. 24, Di's first solo interview was seen as an extraordinary drama that eclipsed Charles's 1994 interview

on ITN with journalist Jonathan Dimbleby. Bold and wide-ranging, Di's talk marked a new era in her turbulent relationship with the Palace—which, ironically, had taken pains of late to reestablish her as a working royal. Aired in Britain on the Queen's 48th wedding anniversary and announced by the BBC on Nov. 14—Charles's 47th birthday—the 55-minute session was interpreted as a hostile gesture not only toward the prince but also to the clan that Di once, in a recorded phone chat with chum James Gilbey, indiscreetly referred to as "this f------ family." Saying she does not expect to become queen and doubts that Charles wants to be king, she claimed that courtiers had pegged her as a troubled woman and "a threat." Still, she said, "I'll fight to the end, because I believe I have a role to fulfill, and I've got two children to bring up."

I've never encouraged the media. There was a relationship which worked before, but now I can't tolerate it because it's become abusive.

—Diana, on her relationship with the media

MARTIN BASHIR INTERVIEW WITH DIANA

MARTIN BASHIR: Your Royal Highness, how prepared were you for the pressures that came with marrying into the royal family?
DIANA: I desperately loved my husband and I wanted to share everything together.

BASHIR: It's been suggested in some newspapers that you were left largely to cope with your new status on your own.
DIANA: You had to either sink or swim. And you had to learn that very fast.

BASHIR: What was the family's reaction to your postnatal depression?
DIANA: Well, it gave everybody a wonderful new label—Diana's unstable and Diana's mentally unbalanced. And unfortunately that seems to have stuck on and off over the years.

BASHIR: According to press reports, it was suggested that it was around this time things became so difficult that you actually tried to injure yourself.
DIANA: You have so much pain inside yourself that you try and hurt yourself on the outside because you want help. . . .

BASHIR: What effect did [your discovery of your husband's relationship with Camilla Parker-Bowles] have on you?
DIANA: Pretty devastating. Rampant bulimia, if you can have rampant bulimia, and just a feeling of being no good at anything and being useless and hopeless and failed in every direction.

BASHIR: Do you think Mrs. Parker-Bowles was a factor in the breakdown of your marriage?
DIANA: Well, there were three of us in this marriage, so it was a bit crowded.

BASHIR: Do you think you will ever be Queen?
DIANA: No, I don't, no.

BASHIR: Why do you think that?
DIANA: I'd like to be a queen of people's hearts, in people's hearts, but I don't see myself being Queen of this country.

Diana admitted falling in love with Capt. James Hewitt (right). "But," she said, "I was very let down."

Diana confessed having "rampant bulimia" after Camilla (far right) became involved with Charles again.

"I'm not really on my own, I've got wonderful friends—I've got my boys," said Diana (below, with Harry, Wills and Charles in August).

" She has to be treated with sufficient respect not to tarnish the crown, but that's all

—author Lady Colin Campbell, on how the Windsors will treat Diana after the divorce

MARCH 11, 1996

Peopl

HER FUTURE BEGINS
DI-VORCE!

$2.59

0 70989 10227 9

11

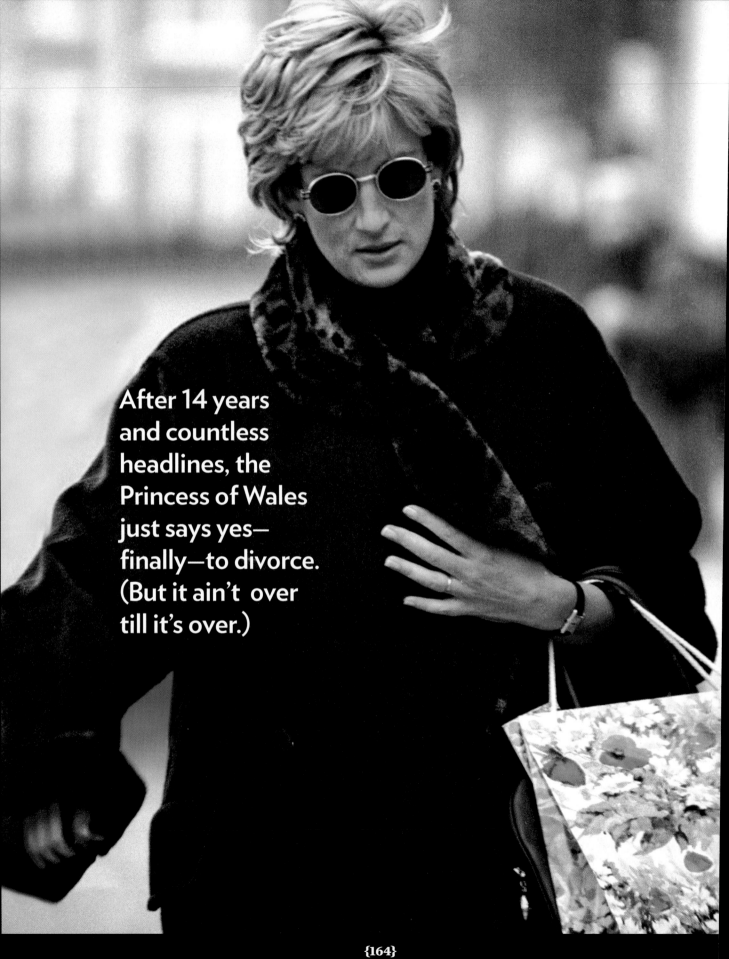

After 14 years and countless headlines, the Princess of Wales just says yes—finally—to divorce. (But it ain't over till it's over.)

PRINCE-LESS DIANA

IN THE END, it seemed, the Prince and the Princess of Wales couldn't present a united front even after they abandoned their torturous marriage. At 6:15 p.m. on Feb. 28, the announcement came not from the Palace, but from one Jane Atkinson, who has been the princess's PR woman for just over a month. In a statement, Atkinson reported that her client had "agreed to Prince Charles's request for a divorce." Apparently determined to remind the world that "I won't go quietly," as she had put it in her defiant interview with the BBC last November, Diana, 34, let it be known that she had arranged to remain at Kensington Palace; that she would "continue to be involved in all decisions" about Prince William, 13, and Prince Harry, 11; and that she would not leave the marriage without a title: "Diana, Princess of Wales."

The move took the Palace by surprise. While Diana had, indeed, met with Charles, 47, at about 5 p.m., courtiers had no idea she would beat them to the press. "The first they knew was when they heard news reports," says author Brian Hoey. Since the Queen, Charles, Prince Andrew and Princess Anne had attended a memorial service for Gulf War veterans at St. Paul's Cathedral earlier in the day, adds Hoey, "they thought they'd get marvelous coverage. Instead, they were upstaged again." Diana had told her sons about the decision earlier in the day. Afterward, says Hoey, "she went straight to St. James's Palace." There, he says, "she saw Charles alone—insisting it was a very private matter and that no one else be there, even though Charles had wanted a third person taking notes."

The pressure of divorce sent Diana into sobs in December, but by February (left) she seemed resigned to her fate and was facing photographers with renewed style.

•JUNE 17 1996•

SPE**DOUBLE ISSUE**

ROCK 'N' ROLL THEN & NOW

JUNE 17, 1996

People

weekly

DI WOWS CHICAGO

Putting aside her bitter divorce, a radiant princess lights up the Windy City

SOME KIND OF MAGIC

Divorce or no, a rousing royal visit to raise money for cancer research proves Chicago is a Di kind of town

S O SHE'LL NEVER be Queen of England. And the Palace may yet quash her announced hopes of becoming "queen of people's hearts." But if it's any consolation to the soon-to-be-ex-Royal Highness, her charity breeze through Chicago last week made one thing crystal clear: In the heartland, Di rules.

You might think average Americans had had their fill of the whiny Windsors. But then Diana shows up on the doorstep, and otherwise rational people suddenly go all goofy. "All she has to do is just stand there and wave, and people go nuts," says Northwestern University sophomore Robert McGuire, 20, who braved a rainy afternoon to meet the princess during her June 4 visit to the school's Evanston, Ill., campus. "She was walking down and shaking hands, and people were jumping up and down. I saw people crying. I mean, for some people this is the best thing they'll ever do in their life. It might be in mine!"

Surrounded by fans, the princess (at the June 5 gala) showed her skill at working the crowd. The 500 journalists who covered her visit wore security tags with Di's likeness (inset).

" Fergie . . . really is her own worst enemy; whereas Diana appears not to be able to do a thing wrong

—author and Windsor watcher Brian Hoey

HOWARD STERN's big-screen reve

BRANDY AND TONI DO THE GRAMMYS!

MARCH 17, 1997

People
weekly

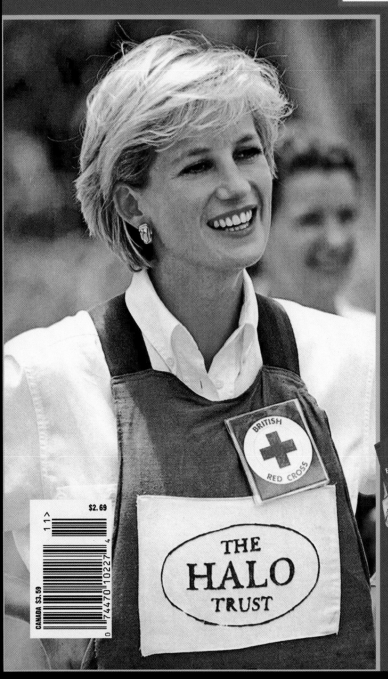

$2.69

CANADA $3.59

0 74470 10227 4

11>

BRITISH RED CROSS

THE HALO TRUST

DIANA & FERGIE

CLASS vs. CASH

Rebounding from their disastrous marriages, Di plays do-gooder while debt-ridden Fergie says, 'Show me the money!'

Diana on a goodwill mission to Angola in January; Fergie hawking her autobiography in Vienna last month

Palace watchers predict that Di (in Angola, Jan. 14) will make more expeditions to the Third World.

HEART AND

Diana devotes herself to good works while free-spending Fergie tries her hand at fattening the bottom line

O N FEB. 11 the British public got a look at a side of Princess Diana that few had expected to see. That evening, the BBC featured a documentary about Diana's January trip to Angola on behalf of the Red Cross. Wearing jeans and little jewelry, she was seen communing with men, women and children whose bodies were shattered by land mines during that country's 20-year civil war. "Treading the delicate line between sympathy and pity," as London's *Daily Mail* observed, Diana inspected a minefield, embraced amputees and comforted a girl recovering from an explosion that tore through her intestines. "That was very traumatic, as a mother, to witness," Diana told the BBC. "Before I came to Angola, I knew the facts. But the reality was a shock."

Days earlier, Diana's erstwhile sister-in-law opened a window on her own life during a visit to Austria. The guest of flamboyant construction magnate Richard Lugner, who lured her to Vienna with a reported $40,000 fee, the Duchess of York was serenaded by a band playing "God Save the Queen" when she emerged from a limo at his shopping complex, Lugner City, for a signing of her autobiography, *My Story*. That evening she attended the Opera Ball with Lugner and his fourth wife. As cameras clicked, she traded pleasantries with Lugner cronies including Jorg Haider, who leads the far-right Freedom Party. A Socialist Party spokesman noted, "Perhaps it was not so easy for her to say no [to Haider] because she was being paid."

Di, in a Catherine Walker, struck an elegant note at a London premiere.

COMMERCE

40

•AUGUST 25 1997•

AUGUST 25, 1997

People

weekly

A GUY FOR DI

In her first real post-Charles romance, Diana takes up with a controversial playboy. Is he a dreamboat—or a deadbeat?

DODI AL FAYED

34>

$2.69

CANADA $3.59

0 74470 10227 4

He's single, he's charming, he's *very* rich. But international playboy Dodi Al Fayed likes to play the field, and Di watchers are wondering if her relationship with him is dalliance or destiny

HOWDY, DODI!

T HE TWOSOME AT the corner table at Paris's cas Carton restaurant on July were smiling and looking axed as they lingered over their ee-star feast. She was blonde, morous and instantly recogniz-e; he, dark-haired, handsome d harder to place. "They cer-nly seemed to be enjoying mselves," says Eventhia nderens, the wife of chef Alain nderens. "When famous people

Di (on the yacht *Jonikal* with Wills and Dodi) reportedly cried when her Saint-Tropez trip ended.

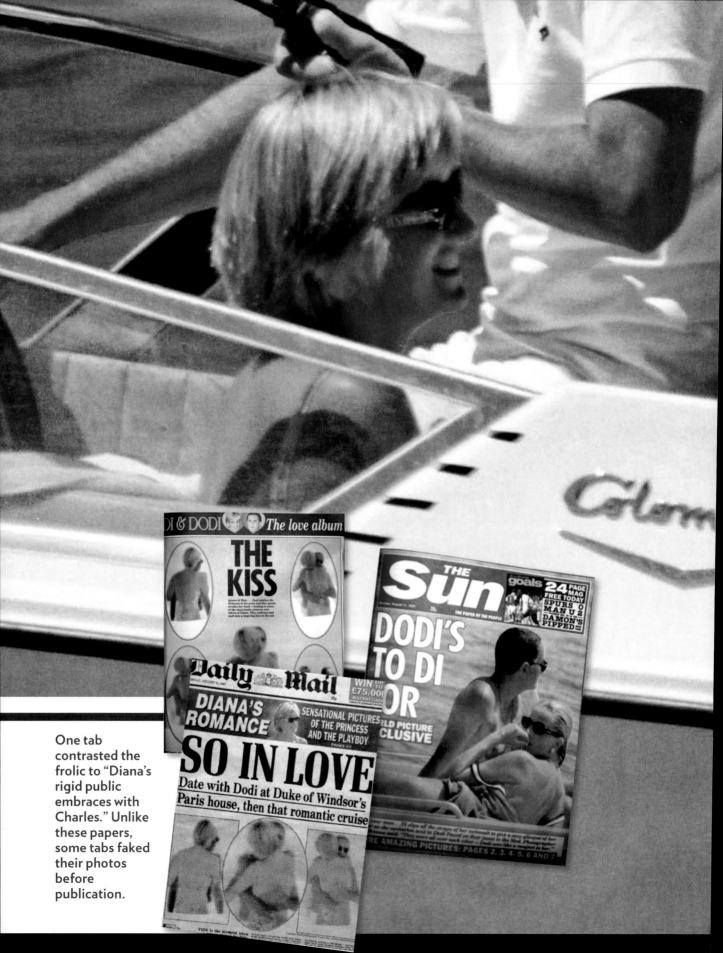

One tab contrasted the frolic to "Diana's rigid public embraces with Charles." Unlike these papers, some tabs faked their photos before publication.

come, you're not constantly bothering them to see if everything's all right. Other customers must have recognized her, but there was no fuss. They were left alone."

Not for long. Two weeks after Princess Di and her mystery date dined à deux, Britain's *Sunday Mirror* published a series of photographs taken off the coast of Sardinia. The pictures broadcast a message as clear as the island's blue waters: A year after her messy divorce from Prince Charles, the world's most eligible princess has a new man. Snapped by an Italian paparazzo, the shots show Di, 36, and Dodi Al Fayed, the 42-year-old son of Harrods owner Mohamed Al Fayed, cuddling aboard Dad's $32 million yacht on Aug. 4. ("You only have to look at the sensual body language," read *The Sunday Mirror*'s overheated prose, "to know that they have found physical and spiritual fulfillment in each other.")

It was the first time since the divorce that she had gone off with a man alone, and for once Di was denying nothing. "She's not reacting in the way she has in the past, by getting upset [at the reports]," says the *Daily Mail*'s Richard Kay. "Dodi has obviously said to her, 'Look, I don't care about the publicity,' so she can relax. And why shouldn't she? She's single, he's single. They like each other."

PART SIX

FAREWELL

SEPTEMBER 15, 1997

People weekly

" Diana was as happy as I have ever known her. For the first time in years, all was well with her world

—journalist friend Richard Kay, whom Di telephoned the evening of Aug. 30, hours before she died

TAKEN TOO

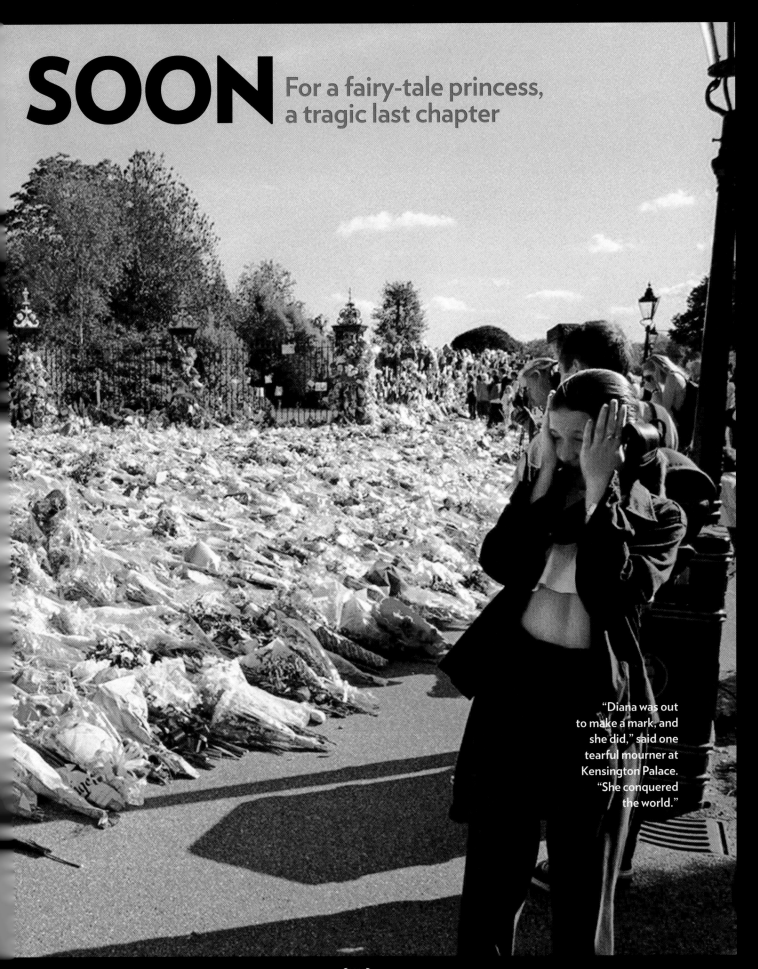

SOON
For a fairy-tale princess, a tragic last chapter

"Diana was out to make a mark, and she did," said one tearful mourner at Kensington Palace. "She conquered the world."

She was born to privilege and wed into royalty—but her real gift was simple compassion. At her death, people the world over turned out to mourn Diana, the woman they loved

T O HER EX-HUSBAND, Prince Charles—as well as to the rest of the world—the death of Diana, Princess of Wales, was an unimaginable shock. On Sept. 1, the day after Diana, 36, and her companion Dodi Al Fayed, 42, died in a cataclysmic car crash in Paris, the distraught Charles walked the hills surrounding Balmoral, the Queen's castle in Scotland. According to Britain's *Daily Mail,* the prince, 48, who had consoled himself with stiff martinis and late-night calls to friends including his mistress, Camilla Parker Bowles, was spotted wandering alone at 6:30 a.m. under dour gray skies. "No one," wrote the *Mail*'s Geoffrey Levy and Richard Kay, "has seen him racked with such a sense of frustration and confusion. . . . Over and over he asked himself how it could be that the fresh and uncomplicated girl he married when

Di and Dodi arrived in Paris Aug. 30 (above). A distraught Charles (left) "will have to put [his sons] first," says author Anthony Holden. "He's all they have." The princess's casket was flown to Britain beneath a flag of the monarchy (far left).

she was 20 should end her life in the mangled wreck of a car speeding through Paris."

With Diana's body lying in the Chapel Royal at St. James's Palace, the world seemed to be pondering the same question. If ever a life had seemed destined for greater things, it was Diana's. In the words of designer Elizabeth Emanuel, who created the princess's 1981 wedding dress, "She wasn't meant to go now; she had such an incredible amount to give still." As the Lord Chamberlain's office and the Spencer family finalized plans for Diana's Sept. 6 funeral at Westminster Abbey (a rite that would include people whom she had touched through her charity work) and her private burial at her family church in Northamptonshire, her admirers were swept up in grief. And there was anger as well—at the paparazzi who pursued the Mercedes in which she and Al Fayed had been riding; at the driver, a Ritz Hotel employee who, according to investigators, was legally drunk when the car flew out of control at a reported 121 mph; and at the press in general, whom many blamed for the death of a woman who lost all claim to privacy when she became a princess.

42

•SEPTEMBER 22 1997•

SPEC
49-PAGE S

SEPTEMBER 22, 1997

People weekly

GOODBYE, DIANA

DIANA

$3.95

■ THE EMOTIONAL FUNERAL ■ HER BROTHER'S BRAVE EULOGY ■ WILLIAM AND HARRY'S FUTURE

" Diana profoundly influenced this nation and the world. She was someone for whom, from afar, we dared to feel affection

—the Very Rev. Dr. Wesley Carr in his opening remarks at Westminster Abbey

FUNERAL
of
DIANA
PRINCESS OF WALES

Saturday 6 September 1997
11.00 a.m.

This 13-page funeral program included full text of the Scripture quoted during the ceremony, as well as the hymns and songs performed by the choir of Westminster Abbey.

"The Queen of Hearts—that's Lady Di for you," said one of countless grieving Britons (above). "Just look around you."

"He has a deep love for the boys," royals author Brian Hoey says of Charles (left, with Harry outside Balmoral Castle).

LOST PRINCESS

With a mixture of pomp, passion and profound sadness, England lays to rest Diana, its cherished rose, as the world watches and weeps

THEY HAD WALKED in its shadow before, down sniper-scarred streets, but these dozen Welsh Guards had never imagined their next experience with death would come on a sun-kissed September morning in London. Still, there was no mistaking the mission that had summoned them from patrol duty in Northern Ireland to the Wellington Barracks in St. John's Wood. Hoisting the 560-lb. practice casket onto their shoulders, rehearsing their stately funereal lockstep, they were preparing for the longest 110 yards of their lives—serving as pallbearers for Princess Diana.

"He was proud to carry her coffin," says Anita Jones, whose son John, 25, was among the members of the 1st Battalion selected by their commanding officer for the assignment. "But he phoned the day before the funeral and told me he was worried. He was afraid that when he saw the people crying, that it would be hard to keep his composure."

And so it was, as became apparent to the 1,900 mourners packing Westminster Abbey Sept. 6 and the more than 2 billion television viewers—the largest audience in TV history—who joined them. "Those poor guardsmen; they looked so desolate and struggling," says David Leonard, who attended the service as a representative of the London Symphony Chorus, of which the princess had been patron. Despite all the days of preparation, neither John Jones and his comrades nor the sorrowful world that watched had been able to anticipate the weight of the solemn spectacle. "I can't believe the strength of the shock," says royal authority Brian Hoey. "Diana will become the Evita of Britain. She will always be a 36-year-old fantasy princess with whom people will identify forever."

Welsh Guards escorted the fallen princess on her final journey.

DIANA
PRINCESS OF WALES

1961-1997

66 I stand before you today the representative of a family in grief, in a country in mourning before a world in shock. We are all united not only in our desire to pay our respects to Diana but rather in our need to do so. For such was her extraordinary appeal that the tens of millions of people taking part in this service all over the world via television and radio who never actually met her, feel that they, too, lost someone close to them in the early hours of Sunday morning. It is a more remarkable tribute to Diana than I can ever hope to offer her today."

—from Earl Spencer's eulogy for his sister,

SEPTEMBER 6, 1997

CREDITS

FRONT COVER
Gamma

CONTENTS
2-3 Glenn Harvey

INTRO
4 AP

PART ONE:
THE FAIRY TALE

6-7 Rex USA; 11 Terry Fincher/Getty; 12-13 (from left) Hulton-Deutsch Collection/Corbis; Tim Graham/Corbis; 16 Rex USA; 19 Camera Press/Retna; 20 Rex USA; 21 Patrick Lichfield/Camera Press; 22 AP; 23 (from top) PA/Empics; Terry Smith (4)

PART TWO:
THE LITTLE PRINCES

24-25 Kim Knott/Camera Press/Retna; 28 (from left) Hulton Archive/Getty; Baron/Camera Press/Retna; 29 PA/Empics; 32 Bettmann/Corbis; 33 Francis Dias/Newspix; 36 Snowdon/Camera Press/Retna; 37 (from top) Mary Evans Picture Library; Mansell Collection/Time Picture Collection; 40 Angeli (2); 41 Time Picture Collection; 44 Jim Bennett/Alpha/Globe; 45 PA/Empics; 47 Jim Bennett/Nunn Syndication; 48 Snowdon/Camera Press/Retna; 49 Camera Press/Retna; 52-53 (from left) Alpha/Globe; Tim Graham/Getty (3); Glenn Harvey/Camera Press/Retna

PART THREE:
CRACKS IN THE AMORE

54-55 Tim Graham; 58 (clockwise from top) Tim Graham/Getty; Getty; Tim Graham/Corbis Sygma; 59 (from left) Tim Graham/Corbis; David Levenson/Getty; Corbis/Sygma; 61 (from top) Tim Graham/Getty; Mauro Carraro/Rex USA/Glenn Harvey/Camera Press/Retna; Jayne Fincher/Princess Diana Archive/Getty; Tim Graham/Getty; 62 Glenn Harvey/Camera Press/Retna; 63 PA/Empics; 65 Alpha/Globe; 66 Nunn Syndication; 69 Ken Goff/INF; 71 Tim Graham/Getty; 72 Mauro Carraro/Rex USA; 73 (clockwise from top left) Tim Graham/Corbis; Glenn Harvey/Camera Press/Retna; Rex USA; 76 Corbis Sygma; 77 Tim Graham/Getty; 79 Jayne Fincher/Princess Diana Archive/Getty; 80 (from top) Hulton Archive/Getty; Globe; 81 Hulton Archive/Getty; 84 RDR/Rex USA; 85 (from left) Rex USA; Tim Graham/Getty; 87 (from top) Tim Graham/Getty; News (UK) Ltd/Rex USA; 89 A.G. Carrick/Diana Memorial Fund/Getty; 90 (from top) Jim Bennett/Nunn Syndication; Clive Postlethwaite/Rex USA; 91 Alpha/Globe; 94 News Group/Rex USA

PART FOUR:
THINGS FALL APART

96-97 Tim Graham; 99 Bryn Colton/Rex USA; 100 (from top) Camera Press/Retna; Retna; Spen/AL/Camera Press/Retna; 101 (clockwise from left) Spen/AL/Camera Press/Retna (2); Rex USA; 104-105 (clockwise from bottom) Sipa; Matthew Polak/Corbis Sygma; David Hartley/Rex USA; Dave Chancellor/Alpha/Globe; 108 (from left) Tim Graham/Getty; Alpha/Globe; Tim Graham/Corbis Sygma; 109 Dave Chancellor/Alpha/Globe; 112 News Group/Rex USA; 113 Camera Press/Retna; 117 Rex USA; 118 PA/Empics; 119 (from left) Nunn Syndication; PA; 122 PA

PART FIVE:
AN INDEPENDENT WOMAN

124-125 Stephane Cardinale/Corbis Sygma; 128 PA/Empics; 129 David Hartley/Rex USA; 132-133 Brendan Beirne/Rex USA; 134 (from top) Christos Zambounis/Gamma; Alpha/Globe; 135 Tim Graham/Corbis; 138 PA/Empics; 141 AP; 142-143 Rex USA (5); 145 Solo/Zuma; 148 Fergus Greer/Getty; 149 (from left) Alpha/Globe; News Group; 151 (from top) Central TV/Corbis Sygma; Arthur Edwards/Camera Press/Retna; 153 Jayne Fincher/Getty; 154-155 (from left) PA/Empics; Mark Cuthbert/Nunn Syndication; PA/Empics; 158 BBC Panorama/AP; 160 Malibu Media; 161 (clockwise from top right) PA/Empics (2); David Hartley/Rex USA; 164 Anthony Jones/UK Press; 167 Ken Goff/INF; (inset) Tim Graham/Getty; 170 Corbis Sygma; 171 David Long/Harlequin; 173 Sipa; 174 Angeli

PART SIX:
FAREWELL

176 Gamma; 180-181 Adrian Dennis/AP; (inset) Cherruault/Sipa; 182 Johnny Eggitt/AFP/Getty; 183 (from top) Malibu Media; Reuters; 186 (from top) UK Press; Reuters; 187 Tim Graham; 188-189 Reuters; 190 Jayne Fincher/Getty

Editor Cutler Durkee
Creative Director Rina Migliaccio
Art Director Caroline Bowyer
Picture Editor James Miller
London Bureau Chief Simon Perry
Writer Steve Dougherty
Reporters Shayla Byrd, Hugh McCarten
Copy Editors Ben Harte, Alan Levine, Mary C. Radich, Joanann Scali
Photo Assistants C. Tiffany Lee, Regina Flanagan, Kristy Jell, Su Smith, Amy Gentle
Production Artist Daniel Neuburger
Scanners Brien Foy, Stephen Pabarue
Imaging Romeo Cifelli, Charles Guardino, Jeff Ingledue, Rob Roszkowski
Research Robert Britton (Director), Céline Wojtala (Deputy), David Barbee, Jane Bealer, Sal Covarrúbias, Margery Frohlinger, Charles Nelson, Ean Sheehy, Jack Styczynski, Patrick Yang

TIME INC. HOME ENTERTAINMENT
Publisher Richard Fraiman
General Manager Steven Sandonato
Executive Director, Marketing Services Carol Pittard
Director, Retail & Special Sales Tom Mifsud
Director, New Product Development Peter Harper
Assistant Director, Brand Marketing Laura Adam
Assistant General Counsel Dasha Smith Dwin
Book Production Manager Suzanne Janso
Design & Prepress Manager Anne-Michelle Gallero
Special Thanks to Bozena Bannett, Alexandra Bliss, Glenn Buonocore, Robert Marasco, Brooke McGuire, Jonathan Polsky, Mary Sarro-Waite, Ilene Schreider, Adriana Tierno, Alex Voznesenskiy

ISBN 10: 1-933821-06-X
ISBN 13: 978-1-933821-06-1
Library of Congress number: 2007902448